Beat Your
Depression

D0275694

Hodder Arnold

A MEMBER OF THE HODDER HEADLINE GROUP

Beat Your
Depression

Paul Jenner
Edited by Denise Robertson

Ventures

A MEMBER OF THE HODDER HEADLINE GROUP

Orders: Please contact Bookpoint Ltd, 130 Milton Park, Abingdon,
Oxon OX14 4SB. Telephone: +44 (0) 1235 827720. Fax: +44 (0) 1235
400454. Lines are open 09.00 to 5.00, Monday to Saturday, with a
24-hour message answering service. You can also order through our
website www.hoddereducation.co.uk.

British Library Cataloguing in Publication Data
A catalogue record for this title is available from the British Library.

ISBN-13: 978 0 340 94321 2

First published   2007
Impression number 10 9 8 7 6 5 4 3 2 1
Year   2012 2011 2010 2009 2008 2007

Copyright © 2007; series editor material © Denise Robertson;
author © Paul Jenner

This Morning is an ITV Production for ITV. © ITV Productions
Limited 2007. Licensed by Granada Ventures Ltd. All rights reserved.

Typeset by Transet Limited, Coventry, England.
Printed in Great Britain for Hodder Education, a division of Hodder
Headline, an Hachette Livre UK Company, 338 Euston Road, London,
NW1 3BH, by Cox & Wyman Ltd, Reading, Berkshire.

Hodder Headline's policy is to use papers that are natural, renewable
and recyclable products and made from wood grown in sustainable
forests. The logging and manufacturing processes are expected to
conform to the environmental regulations of the country of origin.

ABOUT THE AUTHORS

Paul Jenner is a writer and journalist with a special interest in happiness, self-fulfilment and lifestyle issues. He is the author and co-author of almost 20 books, including *Au Revoir Angleterre*, *Teach Yourself Great Sex* and *Teach Yourself Happiness*.

Denise Robertson's television career began with *BBC Breakfast Time* in 1984. She has been the resident agony aunt of ITV's *This Morning* for the last 20 years. In that time she has received over 200,000 letters covering a wide range of problems from viewers and from readers of her newspaper and magazine columns. She has written 19 novels and several works of non-fiction. Her autobiography, *Agony: Don't Get Me Started*, was published in paperback by Little Books in July 2007. She is associated with many charities, among them Relate, The Bubble Foundation, Careline and the National Council for the Divorced and Separated.

WHICH PAGE?

I'm confused – should I take antidepressants or see a psychotherapist? *Turn to page 99.*

I've been thinking about suicide a lot recently. *Turn to pages 18 and 146.*

My partner doesn't understand how I can't just snap out of my depression. *Turn to pages 24 and 193*

I'm worried my son might be depressed. *Turn to page 37.*

How long will it be before I get better? *Turn to page 61.*

I'm pregnant and don't want to take antidepressants. *Turn to page 79.*

I'm thinking about seeing a private psychotherapist – where do I start? *Turn to page 96.*

I seem to get very low in the winter months. *Turn to pages 148 and 163.*

This book is dedicated to Zoe and Laura, two very good reasons for not being depressed.

Also, enormous thanks to Victoria Roddam at Hodder Arnold, without whose ceaseless efforts this book would never have become a reality, and to Jenny Organ.

Paul Jenner, 2007

CONTENTS

FOREWORD

By Fern Britton and Phillip Schofield

As presenters of ITV's *This Morning*, over many years we have met many incredible people with many incredible stories to tell. What we have learned is that life can be wonderful but it can also be very hard.

Our phone-ins have generated thousands of calls a day from viewers all over Great Britain looking for suitable advice on a range of subjects. What is very obvious from these calls is that we are not alone with the personal challenges we often face and there is a great need for help in dealing with them. We are always cheered by the follow-up letters and emails from viewers saying how our experts' advice has helped them to turn their lives around.

Over the 20 years *This Morning* has been on air, Denise Robertson, our agony aunt, has regularly offered support and advice to millions of viewers on a huge range of personal problems, and she spends even more time off-screen answering letters, calling those in distress and dealing with questions via the internet. As a result, she is uniquely qualified to edit these books which reflect the common sense and sensitive advice that we provide on the show.

We believe these survival guides will help you to deal with the practical and emotional fall-out caused by issues such as bereavement, relationship break-ups, debt, infertility, addiction, domestic violence and depression.

If you feel that your particular problems are insurmountable – don't! There is always a way to improve your life or at least get yourself on a path towards a new start. If you think you are alone with your problem – don't! Our experience shows that many of us face the same problems but are often reluctant to admit it. You have already made a great start by picking up this book.

We both wish you all the strength and support you need to tackle your own personal problems and sincerely hope that we can help through these books and through our continued work on the programme.

INTRODUCTION

Look up the word 'depression' in the dictionary and it says 'a sunken or depressed area'. When it happens to you, depression is a large, black hole from which you feel there is no escape. I've been there and scary is not a big enough word to describe it. In addition, depression carries an aura of shame. Half the letters to me on the subject say, 'Don't ask me to tell anyone. I feel so ashamed of feeling like this.' 'Helpful' friends or family members say 'Count your blessings' or, worse still, 'Pull yourself together.' Of course there are things you can do to help yourself but true depression is an illness which, in most cases, needs professional help.

How do you distinguish between 'the blues', which affect all of us at times, and true depression? This book will help you decide by discussing and describing symptoms but a rough rule is that 'the blues' don't last very long and depression, if untreated, persists. Sometimes it occurs because you have had a problem like bereavement or losing your job. Sometimes it appears for no reason whatsoever. Reactive depression, the sort with a problem at its roots, is helped enormously by addressing that problem but all types of depression respond to treatment.

Before you can move forward you need to understand what is happening to you. I promise you, you are not going mad or losing your grip. You will not be like this forever. And even if you've been depressed for years and years it is never too late to seek help. My own depression came after a turbulent period in my life. When at last I acknowledged its existence the problems had been dealt with and my life had actually taken a turn for the better but the effects of the trauma remained and I felt total despair. Happily, the treatment worked and I got well. I have never looked back or suffered from depression again but, if it should return, I now know how to beat it. I want to share that knowledge with you and this book has been written to guide you through the steps you need to take and point to sources of help. Start reading now.

Denise Robertson

Part 1: What to Do Right Now

You feel bad and you don't want to feel bad any more. You want to feel better – *now!* With this in mind Part 1 is a stripped-down version of all the information given in the rest of the book and is designed to help you take immediate action. If there's an emergency or if you just can't cope with too much information at the moment then this will help. Unfortunately, there aren't any instant cures for depression. However, used in conjunction with whatever treatment your doctor advises, this book will hopefully set you on the right path.

My doctor advised me to see a psychotherapist for my depression. At the time I hardly knew anything about it but I was keen to give anything a go. So I was really upset when I discovered there was a three-month waiting list for National Health Service treatment in my area. I couldn't afford to go privately and it just seemed so unfair. My son went to the library and came back with some self-help books. I wouldn't have believed that just reading could do any good but by the time I finally got to see the therapist I was already feeling much better.

Anthea

1

I feel hopeless

At this moment you probably feel as if you're inside some kind of black hole. It may seem that you'll never be able to climb back out again. You feel as if you're sliding deeper and deeper down and that the circle of light at the top is getting further and further away. Feeling depressed is alarming, frightening and absolutely horrible. So although it might seem impossible that you could ever feel happy and optimistic again remember this:

Depression can be treated successfully in almost all cases and quite quickly.

Am I depressed?

If you think you're depressed then you almost certainly are and it's an awful feeling. If you're confused or want to check how severe your condition is, then here's a list of the symptoms. Tick all the ones that apply to you:

❏ Tiredness and loss of energy.
❏ Persistent sadness.
❏ Loss of self-confidence and self-esteem.
❏ Difficulty concentrating.
❏ Inability to see a solution to problems.
❏ Endlessly turning over the things that have gone 'wrong' in your life.
❏ Getting irritable or angry without good reason.
❏ Not being able to enjoy things that are usually pleasurable or interesting.
❏ Feeling guilty or worthless.
❏ Having feelings of helplessness and hopelessness; thinking that life isn't worth living.
❏ Feeling that life is unfair and that you have no power to influence events.
❏ Having problems sleeping – difficulties in getting off to sleep, or waking up much earlier than usual.

❏ Experiencing upsetting dreams.

❏ Avoiding other people, sometimes even your close friends.

❏ Finding it hard to function at work/college/school.

❏ Experiencing a loss of appetite or, conversely, eating for comfort.

❏ Experiencing a loss of sex drive and/or sexual problems.

❏ Having physical aches and pains.

❏ Having thoughts about suicide.

❏ Wanting to self-harm.

How you scored

- 0–4 ticks – normal
- 5–6 ticks – mild depression
- 7–10 ticks – moderate depression✗
- 11–15 ticks – severe depression
- 16–20 ticks – extreme depression

Please bear in mind that how you scored is nothing more than an *indication* of your state of mind. This is not a diagnosis. For that you need to see your doctor.

Q: *Am I sad or am I depressed?*

A: According to some psychotherapists, sadness is proportionate to the event, relates to the *reality* of the situation and goes away in a 'normal' amount of time; depression is disproportionate, stems from a *distorted* way of thinking about the event and doesn't go away for an abnormally long time. (*To find out more about the different types of depression and their causes, see Part 2, Chapter 7*).

What can I do right now?

Step 1: Make an appointment

Make an appointment with your doctor now. If you scored 11 or more ticks in the self-test above ask for an urgent appointment. If you've had suicidal thoughts or self-harmed then you need an appointment *at once* (and read the section 'I'm thinking about suicide' on page 18). If you're afraid the doctor will be cross that you're wasting his or her time you couldn't be more wrong. Doctors aren't only there for physical problems and they all understand the seriousness of even mild depression. So don't be embarrassed to explain exactly how you're feeling. Your doctor may suggest antidepressants or psychotherapy or a combination of both and may also propose lifestyle changes. She or he will also check to see if your depression has a physical cause. (*To find out more about antidepressants and psychotherapy, see Part 2, Chapters 3 and 4*).

Will the depression go by itself?

If you don't seek treatment your depression might eventually go away on its own. However, according to the Royal College of Psychiatrists, it takes on average about eight months, so it's unwise to wait in the hope of recovery before seeking help. Your depression might be shorter but, on the other hand, it might last considerably longer. There's no way of knowing, and besides, eight months is an extremely long and unnecessary length of time to be depressed. Also bear in mind that, if left untreated, depression can get worse. Why take the risk? There's absolutely nothing to be gained. So, please, make that phone call or, if you don't feel up to it, ask someone else to phone on your behalf.

> **WARNING**
>
> Never self-medicate with antidepressants bought over the internet. They can have serious side effects and should only be prescribed by a doctor.

Step 2: In the meantime, while you're waiting...

While you're waiting for your appointment (or when you've just begun treatment and are waiting for it to take effect) here are some things you can do to help yourself:

- Treat yourself to the kinds of things, big and small, that have made you happy in the past – some clothes, a CD, a funny DVD, a relaxing bubble bath, a cake, a hike in the woods...

- Tell people close to you. There's no point in trying to hide the situation and admitting how you feel is one of the first steps to getting better.

- Talk over your feelings with a relative or friend. Just sharing your thoughts, emotions and concerns with someone supportive can be a big help. If there's no one to whom you can turn then telephone a helpline. You'll be talking to someone sympathetic who will understand your problems and who, quite likely, has personal experience of depression. (*To find out about helplines see Part 5, Chapter 14*).

- If your depression comes on when the skies are overcast and the days are short you may be suffering from seasonal affective disorder (SAD). Special lamps which reproduce the beneficial effects of the sunlight you're missing can be purchased for around the same price as other quality light fittings (see Part 5, Chapter 15, page 322).

- Try not to reinforce your negative feelings. In other words, as soon as a thought comes into your head such as 'Life isn't worth living' or 'Real love just doesn't exist' or 'There's no hope', don't allow yourself to dwell on it. Imagine instead that those thoughts are not *your* thoughts but the words of someone else and *refuse to listen*. If necessary say out loud: 'Shut up!' And then get on with something else.

- Minimize stress – reassess your schedule and cut out what's unnecessary.

- Ask a relative or friend to be around but not to crowd you.

- Look after yourself. If you really feel you need to sleep and rest a lot then do so. But also make time to get out for some fresh air, sunshine and exercise.

- Exercise. Research has proven that, for example, jogging for 20 to 30 minutes every other day can be as effective as antidepressants. Start with whatever you can manage – a stroll or a dance – and build up from there. (*To find out more about suitable exercise for alleviating depression, see Part 2, Chapter 5.*)

- Eat meals that contain plenty of green, leafy vegetables, complex carbohydrates (such as potatoes and pasta) and oily fish; shell and eat two Brazil nuts per day. It's possible your depression could be linked to a nutritional deficiency which these foods will rectify. (*To find out more about foods that combat depression see Part 2, Chapter 5.*)

- Avoid alcohol or, at least, cut down.

- Avoid recreational drugs.

- If you've recently begun a new medication check to see if depression could be a side effect.

- If you know that something somebody did or said triggered your depression then discuss it with her or him – or at least discuss the situation with someone you trust.

- If you're depressed about the state of the world try to avoid the grimmer items in the news.

- Try to hold on to the following thought:

I will get better.

I was always expecting other people to cure me and they never did. Then a doctor told me I would never get better unless I helped myself as well. That was the beginning of the end of my depression.

Dean

Step 3: Then, later:

- Ask a relative or friend to accompany you to appointments with the doctor or therapist.

- If you have trouble remembering to take any medicine that's been prescribed ask a relative or friend to take charge of issuing it at the proper time.

- Learn as much as possible about depression. *(For other sources of information, see Part 5.)*

- Talk about your feelings.

- Try to establish something of a daily routine that will give you a structure and sense of purpose without destroying spontaneity.

- Make an effort to do the things you used to enjoy.

- Try to build up the amount of exercise you take each day. Exercise increases endorphins in the body, which are chemicals that make you feel good.

- Try to maintain a regular sex life (solo or with your partner). Sex is particularly important because it's another effective way of increasing endorphins. However, older men in particular should beware of ejaculating too often which can lead to a 'sexual hangover' that actually intensifies depression.

- Don't fear being 'taken over' by help. You'll always remain in charge of your own life.

Q. What are endorphins?

A. Endorphins are chemicals naturally produced in the body. They:
- Boost the immune system and assist healing.
- Reduce the sensation of pain.
- Create the sensations of pleasure, well-being, happiness and bliss.

I'm thinking about suicide

If you've ticked 19 or 20 items in the checklist on pages 8–9 then, please, contact your doctor immediately. You could also ring a helpline such as the Samaritans (see Part 5, Chapter 14) on 08457 90 90 90. Failing that, tell someone close to you *at once* and ask them to contact your doctor without delay. Please try to remember that these terrible suicidal thoughts are caused by your depression – they're NOT a realistic or logical solution to the problems in your life.

Even though you might feel your life is worthless remember that there are other people who don't agree. They love you. When someone takes their own life, they don't just kill themselves, they kill something inside all of the people who love them. Please, try to hang on to that thought. **Many millions of people who have been through what you're feeling are now enjoying life again** and are very, very pleased indeed that they're alive.

Q. If I've got depression does it mean I'll always be a depressive?

A. The statistics do show that someone who has once suffered from depression is quite likely to suffer again. However, the majority of people with depression never have proper treatment. As long as you get proper treatment this time and follow the advice in this book you'll significantly decrease the chances of suffering from depression again but, if you do, the techniques you'll learn this time will make you better able to cope.

MYTH: Depression is a sign of weakness.

FACT: There's absolutely no need to feel ashamed about having depression. It isn't a sign of weakness. Winston Churchill sometimes suffered from 'black dog' and so did the macho writer Ernest Hemingway, but no one would ever have accused them of being weak.

The competition for the top positions at work was intense and I was drinking heavily to help me cope. I suppose it was inevitable I'd be caught for drink driving sooner or later but when it happened I was devastated. I told myself it proved how worthless I was. I actually welcomed all the punishment I got, including a one-year driving ban because I wanted to suffer as much as possible. Even though I was a senior executive and could have had a chauffeur I insisted on going everywhere on foot and by bus. And the drinking just got worse. Of course, I didn't get one of the top jobs. In fact, I got the sack and became even more depressed. It was only then I sought help. A therapist saved me. She made me realize I didn't have to be top. I stopped drinking and took a job with less pressure. My husband and kids are much happier now. I've learned that's worth far more than being number one at work.

Jill

Could I have bipolar disorder?

Rather than being constantly depressed, some people swing from one extreme to the other. They describe living a kind of roller-coaster, from depression to euphoria and back again. Fortunately, there are treatments that are highly effective.

Tick any of the following symptoms that apply to you:

❏ You feel euphoric and full of energy.

❏ You barely stop to eat or sleep.

❏ Anything is possible.

❏ You get irritable with people who can't keep up with you.

❏ You get angry if anyone disagrees with you.

If you ticked three or more you might be in the 'up phase' of bipolar disorder or, as it used to be called, manic depression, and you should consult your doctor.

Things that can help in a manic phase:

- Relax. (*Some relaxation techniques are explained in Chapter 8 and there's also a quick-reference guide in Part 5, Chapter 12.*)

- Take exercise.

- Try to focus your energy on things like writing, painting, sculpting or carpentry.

- Do your best to eat healthily, which means cutting down on junk foods, processed foods, additives, drinks containing caffeine (such as tea, coffee and cola) and alcohol.

- Stop taking drugs not prescribed by a doctor.

- Try to defer important decisions until you can consider them in a more balanced way.

- Walk away from arguments.

- Ask everyone to ignore silly things you say.

- Even if you can't sleep at night, at least try to make yourself comfortable and relax for a bit, perhaps with a book.

Q: What is bipolar disorder (manic depression)?

A: It's an illness that causes sufferers to swing between very low moods (depression) and periods of very excited, overactive behaviour (mania).

If you want to make it right, write

Why don't you write down what you feel? It can really help. Describe your problems, yourself, the people you come into contact with and the world in general. Go for it and don't hold anything back.

Write good things down too. Maybe you feel your partner doesn't love you, but can you also think of some good things they've done for you?

Write every day, even several times a day, if you want.

My family and friends don't understand

Your family and friends are probably finding it very difficult to understand what you're going through. Quite possibly they're saying things like:

- 'What's the matter with you?'
- 'Pull yourself together.'
- 'Snap out of it.'
- 'Stop being so self-indulgent.'

If that's the case, try not to blame them. If you had a broken leg they'd be able to see the problem, but they can't 'see' depression, only what it does to you – and them. Why not ask them to read this book? And remember:

It's not only you that needs understanding, it's also your loved ones.

Loving your partner

If you're married or living with someone then your depression will be having a significant impact on your partner as well.

- Be honest. Admit you're suffering from depression.

- Don't try to hide it. If you do, your partner may completely misinterpret your behaviour.

- Explain how you're feeling and let your partner discuss his or her concerns, too.

- If your depression is severe you may need to ask your partner to take on responsibility for some or all of the things you would normally do.

Even getting better can cause its own problems – it may take time for your partner to readjust to your new way of thinking and behaving. This is therefore going to be a difficult period for your relationship and it may be a good idea to consider relationship counselling. (*To find out more about relationship counselling, see Part 5.*)

Loving your children

If you have children, don't forget that they may also be affected by your depression.

- Be as honest as you can – if your children see that you're troubled but don't know why they may invent even worse reasons.

- Do your best to show that you still love them.

- Reassure them that they will be looked after.

- Make sure they don't feel guilty. (Children often blame themselves when there are problems: 'Mummy/Daddy wouldn't be like this if I hadn't been naughty.')

- Don't feel guilty yourself because you can't do as much with the children as you would like.

- Ask your children to prioritize things they'd like you to do with them and begin with the first thing on the list. If you can do more, great! If not, one is better than nothing.

- You may have to ask your children for help with chores they wouldn't normally do.

MYTH: Alcohol can cheer you up if you're depressed.

FACT: In reality, alcohol is a depressant. People who are happy are more likely to show their happiness when they drink because alcohol also reduces inhibition. However, if you're already depressed alcohol will only make you feel worse.

Hang in there

Unfortunately, no one has yet found a way of bringing an instant end to depression. So hang in there until the things in this book have had a chance to work. Take courage from the fact that other people have been there before you and have come through it.

2

I'm worried about someone close to me

Living with someone who has depression
is alarming and worrying and if they're
talking about suicide it becomes a very
frightening situation indeed. You're going
to need super-normal patience – but it will
pay off. You're also going to need a lot of
emotional support and practical help from
friends and family. Don't be afraid to ask
for it and, above all, don't be afraid of the
future. **Things will work out.**

How to help NOW

Bear in mind that during an initial crisis the primary aim is simply to get through until professional treatment is available.

Step 1

- Don't 'sulk back' at the person you're worried about but try to be calm, centred and rational.

- Be sympathetic; say that you understand.

- Help remove all pressure and stress from your loved one's life – cancel appointments, deal with problems.

- Never leave a seriously depressed person alone but, on the other hand, don't crowd her or him.

- If your loved one needs a lot of sleep and rest then that's fine. However, also do your best to encourage exercise because it can be at least as effective as antidepressants. (*To find out more about exercise as a treatment for depression, see Part 2, Chapter 5.*)

- Encourage healthy eating. Meals should include fresh green leafy vegetables, complex carbohydrates (such as potatoes and pasta) and oily fish. Shell a couple of Brazil nuts each day. (*To find out more about food as a treatment for depression, see Part 2, Chapter 5*).

- If the state of the world could be linked to the depression then cut down on news.

- Ask your loved one what she or he *needs* and do your best to provide it; don't impose your ideas.

- Discourage alcohol and recreational drugs.

- Check any new medication – depression could be a side effect.

- Make sure that you, also, have someone to support you at this difficult time.

Step 2: Then, in the following days...

- Give moral support by accompanying your loved one to appointments with the doctor or therapist.

- Try to make sure the prescribed treatment is followed correctly.

- Learn as much as possible about depression. (*To find out more about the different kinds of depression and their causes, see Part 2, Chapter 7. For other sources of information, see Part 5.*)

- Be a good listener. Be willing to hear about your loved one's *feelings*.

- Be a good talker. Say how much you love and admire him or her and say why.

- Encourage your loved one to follow a daily routine but allow room for spontaneity.

- Encourage your loved one to return to the things he or she used to enjoy doing.

- Encourage a gradual increase in daily exercise because it increases endorphins in the body, which are the chemicals that make us all feel good.

REMINDER

Endorphins are chemicals that make us feel good (see Chapter 1, page 17).

- If it's your partner who is depressed, try to show that you're nevertheless still interested in sex (unless sex is one of the things he or she has a problem with). Sex is particularly important because it's one of the most effective ways of increasing endorphins. However, older men in particular should be aware that ejaculating too often could produce a 'sexual hangover' that might make depression worse.

- Try to create little moments of happiness every day – it could just be crumpets for tea or playing a favourite piece of music and dancing together.

What to tell the children

If there are children in the family their needs have to be considered as well. Depending on age and personality they may feel frightened, powerless, anxious, neglected, resentful, angry and much more. However, you can do a lot to cushion them from their father's/mother's depression (but not hide it from them):

- Try to explain what is happening by giving as much information as you think the children can handle.

- Prioritize activities together with the children so at least the most important things are done.

- Try to stick to the pre-depression routines as far as possible.

- Try to stick to the pre-depression discipline as well – don't fall for the old 'Mummy/Daddy would have let me do that' routine.

- Tell teachers about the situation.

- Let the neighbours know if you need their help.

- Make additional child care arrangements with family.

- Work out emergency arrangements in advance. For example, what will happen if a child is sick while you have to go to work and your partner is severely depressed?

- Discuss with the children what they should do in an emergency. For example, they should know what telephone numbers to ring if a depressed parent acts strangely.

- Try to keep up with the treats and outings the children would normally have enjoyed.

- If the children are old enough there's no reason why you shouldn't discuss their father's/mother's depression with them.

- Encourage the children to express their own feelings.

- Encourage the children to take on suitable chores.

Is my child depressed?

The problems of childhood can seem trivial compared to 'adult problems', but don't forget that they're just as overwhelming to children as adult problems are to adults. It's all relative – and, unfortunately, many children *are* caught up in adult problems such as:

- You've been rowing with your partner.

- You're in the process of separation or divorce.

- You have a new partner.

- Someone in the family has died.

And, of course, there are all the other problems of youth, including:

- Exams.

- Bullying.

- Alcohol and drugs.

- Broken hearts.

If your child exhibits some of the symptoms given in the checklist in the previous chapter (pages 8–9) then you're right to be worried about depression. Handle the situation with the same seriousness you would for an adult. The principles of treatment are the same but, in most cases, antidepressant drugs are not used.

REMEMBER

Even after successful treatment your child still needs to keep up with the therapeutic techniques, such as positive thinking, healthy eating and exercise, in order to avoid the possibility of a relapse.

Is my elderly parent depressed?

Although surveys show that people tend to get happier as they progress through their fifties, sixties and seventies, many older people nevertheless have to confront life's most difficult problems such as:

• Money worries.

• The deaths of close friends.

• The death of a partner.

• Living alone.

• Being unable to cope with the house or garden.

• Failing health.

With those kinds of problems it's only natural to be sad at times. However, take a look again at the list of the symptoms of depression in Chapter 1 (pages 8–9). So many of them *seem* to be a normal part of ageing but don't make the mistake of dismissing:

• Loss of energy.

• Difficulty concentrating.

- No longer enjoying the activities that used to bring pleasure.

- Feeling helpless.

- Sleeping problems.

- Loss of appetite.

- Physical aches and pains.

If an older relative is exhibiting these signs don't think 'that's just how older people are'. Several symptoms together could be a sign of depression. Make sure they see a doctor.

Could it be bipolar disorder?

If your loved one has periods of abnormal energy which exhaust you and everybody else then depression may be the last thing on your mind. However, high energy together with extreme self-confidence and rapid, sometimes illogical, speech are symptoms of bipolar disorder (manic depression). In many respects these episodes may not be too damaging and can be extremely creative. The big danger is that the sufferer will make decisions that aren't rational and any attempt by you to talk them out of something reckless may be met by anger and abuse. Eventually, the extreme highs are followed by extreme lows.

Things that may help during a manic phase:

- Try to keep the atmosphere calm; play relaxing music.

- Suggest some positive ways of channelling the energy. Exercise is a good idea, as are activities like writing and painting.

- Discourage junk foods, processed foods, additives and drinks containing caffeine (such as tea, coffee and cola). Provide alternatives.

- Discourage alcohol and any drugs not prescribed by a doctor.

- Don't take any notice of stupid or rude remarks – they're just a result of the illness and don't mean anything. (*To find out more about bipolar disorder, see Part 2, Chapter 7.*)

I'm exhausted by my loved one's depression

Of course, there's another side to this whole subject of helping someone with depression. You, too, are going to need support and understanding. You may not be depressed but you're certainly going to be suffering the effects of your loved one's depression. At times you're going to feel:

- Abandoned.

- Unappreciated.

- Unloved.

- Exhausted.

If you're going to survive you're going to need a combination of good organization, practical help, emotional support and the constant knowledge that depression is an illness that can be cured.

Some things that may help you to cope:

- Don't try to cope entirely on your own. It's too much for one person.

- Enlist the help of relatives, friends and neighbours.

- If there are children in the family, encourage them to help you by taking on suitable, manageable chores. They'll probably be more willing if they can choose what to do and work as a team.

- Prioritize. Don't expect to accomplish everything that used to be accomplished. Start with the most important things and do the best you can. Forget the rest.

- Take advantage of every time-saving measure you can. For example, you might be able to order all your groceries on the internet and have them delivered, or you can double up on recipes and freeze half for another day.

- If your depressed partner used to take care of bills, it may be that you'll need to reorganize finances so that you can make sure they're paid on time.

- Try to make arrangements so you can have some time to yourself and continue to enjoy the things that are most important to you.

- If there's no one else you can turn to, or if you just want to talk things over with people who'll understand, there are special organizations for carers (*see Part 5*).

Can I cure my loved one's depression?

There are always things you can do to *help* cure depression. If the depression is mild and your loved one is sufficiently capable of self-help then, between you, you can make a considerable difference.

Step 1: Discover and avoid the 'trigger'

If you think it's possible that something that happened between the two of you was the trigger for depression then, obviously, you should avoid repeating that trigger.

The slightest criticism from my partner sends me into a depression which lasts for several days. I don't usually say anything. I just go off and brood about it and feel more and more hopeless. Eventually I do get over it but then it happens again. And again. If my partner asks me why I'm depressed she often can't believe the reason I tell her.

> *To her it seems trivial but my*
> *relationship is fundamental to my*
> *happiness so any suggestion it's less*
> *than perfect fills me with despair. I*
> *realize I'm overreacting but I can't seem*
> *to do anything about it.*
>
> **Richard**

Some doctors might say Richard isn't really depressed because he always gets over it quite quickly. On the other hand, his low moods are so frequent that during the course of a year he can be depressed for several months. So it's a significant problem that has to be tackled.

Richard and his partner need to do some serious talking and there have to be changes on both sides. His partner, Anna, needs to realize that Richard, reasonably or not, is far more sensitive than most men about certain issues. During the crisis period, until Richard has been successfully treated, she should avoid saying the kinds of things that trigger him.

In the longer term, Richard has to understand that one criticism doesn't mean Anna doesn't love him. But above all, rather than sulking, Richard needs to learn to raise the subject *immediately*.

When he goes off and broods, the problem becomes magnified in his mind – 'She wouldn't say that if she loved me. This relationship is just a sham.' And so on. By talking it through as soon as it happens the issue can be seen in its proper perspective.

Step 2: Listen and talk

Using the techniques in this book you may be able to act the role of therapist. However, please remember that anything more than *mild* depression always requires the help of an expert.

- Be certain you've read the book thoroughly and understand what needs to be done.

- Sometimes a problem lies behind depressive behaviour, so, if you know that something that happened between you was the trigger then try to make your loved one see that whatever was said or done wasn't meant in the way it's been taken. If the trigger concerns other people, discuss the problem and see if, between you, you can work out the best thing to do.

- Always try to be calm and logical. Let your partner see that there's an oasis of tranquillity (you) to which they can return.

Someone close is talking about suicide

Many people don't know how to respond to somebody who talks of feeling suicidal. But don't imagine that talking about suicide encourages suicide. The opposite is the case. If someone you know says they want to die then, please, talk to them about it. Don't change the subject.

If you believe someone is contemplating suicide contact the doctor immediately. You could also phone the Samaritans on 08457 90 90 90 on their behalf (*see Part 5*). So how will you know if suicide is really a possibility? Here are some risk factors:

- Previous suicide attempt.

- Suicide in the family.

- Putting affairs in order (for example, making a will).

- A recent bereavement.

- A major disappointment.

- A sudden change in behaviour (for example, becoming unusually cheerful).

- Talking about suicidal feelings.

- Any of the symptoms of depression listed in Chapter 1 (pages 8–9).

However, don't go jumping to the conclusion that someone is contemplating suicide just because they've, for example, made a new will. But if you see several factors together be vigilant.

One thing you can do is ask your loved one to promise not to try to commit suicide at least until having received treatment. You could even write out a 'contract' on a piece of paper: 'I agree I will not try to commit suicide until I have given treatment a chance for six months', or something like that. Of course, a signature on the contract has no validity but it might just be enough to prevent an attempt.

> *MYTH: People who talk about suicide never do it.*
>
> **FACT:** Among those who commit suicide there are both those who did talk about their suicidal feelings and those who concealed them. The tragedy is that those who give warning of their plans are often ignored. Always take such talk seriously.

You can only do so much

Unfortunately, neither antidepressants nor psychotherapy can bring depression to an immediate end. It all takes time. Don't blame yourself because your loved one isn't getting better instantly. You can only do so much. Remember that many other people have been in your position and come through it. Hold on to this thought:

One day soon my loved one will be happy again and so will I.

Part 2:
Getting Better

This part of the book is divided into five chapters. Together they'll explain to you exactly what depression is, how you get it, how it's treated and the things you can do to help yourself. Hopefully, you'll find here the things that can cure your depression and make you happy once more.

To find out about going to see the doctor and the kinds of treatment that might be suggested, see Chapters 3 and 4.

To find out about things you can do to help yourself, see Chapters 5 and 6.

To find out about the different kinds of depression and their causes, see Chapter 7.

3

What can my doctor do for me?

When you're suffering from depression your doctor is one of the first people you should turn to. In this chapter we're going to take a look at the standard treatments for depression that are available from your general practitioner (GP). If you'd like to know about self-help and alternative treatments then move on to Chapters 5 and 6.

Is depression always treatable?

Yes, depression is always treatable, although some cases need more intense treatment for longer periods than others. Around 80 per cent of sufferers respond positively to a combination of the two standard modern treatments – that's to say, antidepressants and 'talking therapy'.

So the probability of fast, successful treatment is very high. However, if you should be among the 20 per cent who do not respond very strongly then please don't become despondent. Your doctor has several other avenues of approach, including the use of antidepressants in combination. It may take a little longer but you have every reason to be optimistic.

What's more, as you'll see in Chapters 5 and 6, there are various self-help therapies which can be of considerable benefit. In some cases, using just one of those therapies may be enough to cure depression. Using several, together with whatever your doctor advises, arms you with the most powerful depression-busting techniques that are known to date.

Your doctor is likely to offer you one or both of the following:

- Antidepressants.

- Psychotherapy.

Of course, it's always possible your doctor will discover a cause for your condition that requires a very different approach, but these are the standard ones.

Q: What are antidepressants?

A: Antidepressants are medicines that directly return the chemistry of the brain to the way it was before you became ill. The most famous of them all is Prozac but there are very many others.

Q: What is psychotherapy?

A: Psychotherapy or 'talking therapy' aims to return the chemistry of the brain to the way it was before you became ill. It does this indirectly by changing the way you think about your life.

Seeing your doctor

It can be hard to tell your doctor you're suffering from depression, especially if you've been going to the same surgery for years and you feel you've built up a measure of respect. It can also be very difficult for you if you're young. Just remember that your doctor is a professional who is used to dealing with a whole range of problems and is there to help.

Don't worry, either, about gossip getting out into the wider community. Everyone who works at the surgery is bound by the same code of ethics regarding confidentiality.

Depression is an illness and it can have many different causes, including a viral infection. So there's no need to feel any more awkward than if you had the flu. What's more, your doctor may well have suffered from depression in the past – it's a high risk career for depression. If that's the case you can depend on considerable sympathy and insight. So describe the way you feel as fully and accurately as you can. The more information you can give your doctor the better you can be helped.

In the vast majority of cases, it will be your doctor who treats you, probably together with a counsellor who may also work at the surgery. However, if it's felt you'd benefit from more specialist attention you might be referred to a psychiatrist or to the Community Mental Health Team (see page 63). Don't think your doctor is just trying to get rid of you. Your GP is trying to do the best for you.

I think it must have been about three years before I plucked up the courage to go and see the doctor. I wasn't depressed all the time so I was always putting it off. I used to cheer myself up by buying clothes and then I never wore them. Things like that. I could have avoided a lot of problems if I'd just gone sooner.

Rebecca

Q: How long will it take for the doctor to make me better?

A: The average for the disappearance of symptoms is about 13 weeks. However, that doesn't mean you won't have to continue treatment for some time because the doctor needs to be sure the symptoms won't reappear.

Your doctor may recommend psychotherapy alone or antidepressants together with psychotherapy. **Ideally antidepressants should always be used in conjunction with psychotherapy.** The reason for this is that there's a much lower relapse rate when psychotherapy forms part of the treatment. Unfortunately, however, there is a waiting list of several months for psychotherapy in many areas of the country. In reality, therefore, you may find yourself taking antidepressants without the additional benefit of psychotherapy.

MYTH: A psychiatrist is just another name for a psychologist.

FACT: A psychiatrist is a medical doctor who has gone on to specialize in emotional and mental problems, whereas a psychologist is not a medical doctor but someone who has a degree in psychology (the study of human behaviour). Not all psychologists go on to treat patients but might go into research, for example. Psychologists who do treat people are normally called clinical psychologists or chartered psychologists or even chartered clinical psychologists. Psychologists cannot prescribe medication.

Seeing the Community Mental Health Team

The idea of being referred onwards by your doctor can be very worrying. It seems to suggest that there's something seriously wrong with you. Especially when the words 'mental health' are used. Rest assured that there's absolutely no reason to be alarmed. On the contrary. It doesn't mean you're 'too ill' for your doctor to manage alone, it simply means you're fortunate to live in an area where there is a whole range of people with different areas of specialization that can be brought to bear. It makes very good sense. And after all, they had to call the team something. The team usually involves from 8 to 16 people, each with their own area of specialization. In effect, it means your depression can be attacked on several fronts simultaneously.

The team might be based at your GP's surgery or at a day-centre or it might have its own clinic. Members of the team can also visit you in your own home, if appropriate.

To begin with you might just see one person known as the 'key worker'. The key worker is responsible for co-ordinating all the other members of the team and will chat with you in a friendly and easy-going atmosphere to decide on the best way to proceed. The idea is to tackle your depression on several fronts at the same time. As explained later in this chapter and the next, some types of depression respond very well to just one type of treatment but others respond much better to a combination of treatments.

As a result of your chat with your key worker you may then go on to see just one other member of the team or you might see several. Your key worker may also suggest involving your partner or other members of your family. Note the word 'suggest'. Everything between you and the team is confidential and no one can force you to rope in other members of your family against your wishes. However, very often, your relationships with other members of your family may form part of the solution to your problem. Don't forget, also, that your partner or family may themselves need advice, help and support. So, all in all, if the key worker suggests family involvement you can be sure it's believed to be in your best interest.

Rest assured that if you're with the Community Mental Health Team you're in very good hands.

> *Q: Can I contact the CMHT directly without seeing my doctor first?*
>
> **A:** The policy varies from area to area but, generally, you'll have to be referred by your GP. However, some CMHTs can be contacted directly and, in any case, if you're feeling desperate a CMHT will always do what's best for you, whether you've been referred by your GP or not.

Seeing a psychiatrist

It's possible you'll see a psychiatrist as one of the members of the CMHT or, alternatively, your GP might refer you directly to one. A psychiatrist is simply a doctor who specializes in emotional and mental problems such as depression.

There's no need to feel nervous. A psychiatrist is just a normal human being like you. Some psychiatrists may be happy for you to bring a friend or relative with you for your first interview while others may prefer to see you alone. Don't worry about being asked awkward questions straight away. On the contrary, your first interview, which will probably last about an hour, will mostly be concerned with practical matters. The psychiatrist will want to know about your general background, your state of health, any emotional problems you've had in the past and what's going on in your life right now.

Later on, however, the questions may become a little more probing. Understandably, a lot of people resent this. They don't like the idea of a stranger knowing their 'secret' thoughts. In reality, of course, it's when we reveal our innermost thoughts that we show what interesting people we really are. You're far more likely to find the experience exhilarating than anything else.

Not all psychiatrists provide psychotherapy, however. Some specialize far more in medication.

MYTH: If you go to see a psychiatrist you'll end up in a hospital.

FACT: Only about one in every 100 people with depression is ever given any treatment in hospital so it's highly unlikely. However, when hospital is considered the best option most people feel extremely relieved because it's a safe place to be and has the best possible treatment.

Antidepressants

If your doctor suggests antidepressants you may, like many people, immediately feel encouraged that something positive is being done for you. There's often a great sense of relief when you walk out of the surgery with that prescription in your hand. That's already good. On the other hand, you may feel resistant to the whole idea of antidepressants in the belief that they're addictive, involve dangerous chemicals and will rob you of your true personality. So it's important to stress that:

- Most people have no difficulty giving up antidepressants at the appropriate time, under medical supervision.

- Antidepressants are not dangerous in the proper doses.

- Antidepressants are more likely to give you *back* your true personality than steal it.

> *Q: How do antidepressants work?*
>
> **A:** Antidepressants increase the amount of serotonin in the brain, one of the chemicals that can make people feel more contented.

One thing is for sure. If you're enthusiastic about antidepressants they're more likely to work well for you, and if you're strongly against antidepressants they're less likely to help you.

If you are worried by the idea of antidepressants be sure to discuss the subject with your doctor. Explain what you feel. No one can force you to take antidepressants if you don't want to.

If you do have strong objections to antidepressants that certainly doesn't mean the doctor can't do anything for you. GPs have lots of other possibilities. The main one is 'psychotherapy'. If you think psychotherapy is what you'd prefer you'll find full details in Chapter 4.

However, if psychotherapy isn't immediately available in your area do try to overcome your worries about antidepressants. Studies show that around two-thirds of people respond positively to them and by refusing to take them you'll be denying yourself an excellent chance of feeling better. While waiting for psychotherapy you may find helplines beneficial (see Part 5, Chapter 14).

Q: How will I know which is the best antidepressant for me?

A: Deciding that is the doctor's job, but you can help make sure the right decision is reached by providing accurate answers to your doctor's questions. That said, it's still very much a question of 'suck it and see'. If an antidepressant doesn't work for you, or has unbearable side effects, then you'll have to try another. And, if necessary, another.

I suffer from multiple sclerosis. It's been in remission for years but I have to walk with a stick. In the beginning I went to see counsellors who told me I had plenty to be happy about but I'd like to see them swap places with me. I went on antidepressants five years ago and I am sort of happy now.

Helen

What to expect if you take antidepressants

The important thing to keep in mind is that:

Antidepressants do not work at once.

It usually takes two to three weeks for an antidepressant to begin to take effect. It's very important to understand this and not to become despondent if there's no immediate change in your condition, especially if, in the meantime, you're having to put up with side effects. Prozac seems to take even longer, at anything from five to eight weeks. So you need to give an antidepressant a while to prove itself.

On the other hand, if your condition hasn't improved after two months then there's no point in continuing with that particular antidepressant at that dose.

MYTH: The newer antidepressants are obviously better than the older ones.

FACT: The newer and older depressants work equally well but the newer ones tend to have fewer side effects (see below).

Antidepressants and bipolar disorder

If you're suffering from bipolar disorder (manic depression) your doctor is likely to prescribe a mood stabilizer such as lithium. If this is the case, please try to look upon it in a positive way. Don't think: 'It's horrible to have to take this drug for the rest of my life.' Rather, see it this way: 'Thank goodness I'll be able to lead a full and normal life.'

Bipolar disorder is, of course, a chronic (that is, long lasting) condition. However, you have grounds for optimism. A great deal of research is being done, new treatments are being tried experimentally every year, and the outlook for new approaches is very good.

If your manic phases are quite manageable it may be that your doctor will decide a mood stabilizer isn't necessary. He may instead prescribe antidepressants for those periods when you feel down. Be aware, however, that occasionally antidepressants can themselves trigger a manic phase and that it could begin in as little as one to two days after starting the antidepressants.

Q: What should I do if, after taking an antidepressant, I feel a manic phase beginning?

A: Contact your doctor immediately.

The correct antidepressant dose

The correct dose of an antidepressant is vital as an antidepressant may not work if the dose is either too low or too high.

The fact that you don't respond to a particular dose doesn't mean a drug is ineffective. It may well be that the dose will have to be increased or *even reduced*. Twice as much of a drug isn't necessarily twice as good.

With some antidepressants your doctor may tell you to build up gradually to the prescribed dose over a period of one or two weeks. It's nearly always a good idea to follow the same method when coming off antidepressants, too, tapering down the dose over a period.

If you're worried about the whole idea of antidepressants don't make the mistake of taking less than the prescribed dose. That's only going to cause confusion for your doctor. Take the dose as prescribed and then let your doctor assess whether or not it can be reduced.

Antidepressants could transform your life. So hang in there and if, in the end, antidepressants just aren't right for you then at least you'll have tried.

> **As a general rule, the longer you've been taking antidepressants the longer it takes to come off them.**

Q: How long should I take antidepressants for?

A: Different doctors have different ideas but, in general, you should normally aim to be off antidepressants within a year. Some patients are successfully treated in as little as three months. However, there are cases where it's necessary to take antidepressants indefinitely, for example, in the case of bipolar disorder (manic depression) or in the case of long-term, recurrent depression.

Q: What time of day should I take antidepressants?

A: That depends on the particular drug. Discuss this carefully with your doctor. Some antidepressants make you sleepy, in which case it's best to take them at bedtime. Others have the reverse effect and are best taken in the morning. But some have to be taken in several doses and one of those doses may have to be at a less than ideal moment.

Children and antidepressants

Many specialists believe that children under 18 should not be prescribed antidepressants until other methods have first been tried. The fact is that children's bodies just aren't the same as adults' bodies and react differently. Some antidepressants have been linked with an increase in self-harm in young people, suicidal thoughts and, indeed, actual suicide. What's more, some studies suggest that antidepressants alone are usually no more effective than placebos as a treatment for depression in children. In other words, the most successful strategy for children is likely to be a combination of psychotherapy with practical steps to tackle any problems a child may have. However, if your doctor decides to prescribe antidepressants you can be sure it's for a very good reason.

Monitoring your child's antidepressants

It would be a good idea to keep control of the tablets and monitor for the following, especially during the first few months or whenever the dose is increased or decreased:

- Sadness.
- Agitation.
- Anxiety.
- Restlessness.
- Aggression.
- Panic attacks.
- Sleeping problems.
- Becoming very talkative or hyperactive.
- Problems at school.
- Spending a lot of time alone.
- Self-harming.
- Suicidal thoughts.
- A suicide attempt.

Initially, your child should see the doctor every week during the first month and twice during the second month with a follow-up at the end of three months.

Side effects of antidepressants

It's a great shame that a medicine that can be so helpful can also have quite unpleasant side effects. When you're already depressed the last thing you want is to start having headaches or blurred vision or diarrhoea that you didn't have before. So it can be a very frustrating and upsetting time when you first start on an antidepressant. The good news is that the worst side effects usually only last for a week or two. The even better news is that the newer generation of drugs have far fewer side effects than the earlier kinds. In one study, 30 per cent of people on an 'old-style' antidepressant stopped taking the medicine, while in the case of Prozac, one of the newer ones, the drop-out rate was only 10 per cent. So that's a strong argument in favour of the newer antidepressants.

Q: Will the side effects go away?

A: Side effects are generally at their worst during the first few days; after that they tend to taper off.

There are cases of people being convinced they've got all sorts of side effects which, upon investigation, have nothing to do with the antidepressants at all.

The best idea is to write down any problems you may have *before* starting the treatment. Then continue to record side effects at least once a week. That will give you a better idea of what's causing the difficulties. On page 78 there is a quick guide to the kinds of side effects are we talking about.

Q: Is there anything I can do to reduce side effects?

A: If the side effects are severe discuss them with your doctor. Quite often it's possible to reduce the dose and thereby the side effects without reducing the effectiveness of the treatment. But only your doctor can decide.

Possible side effects* of antidepressants

Tricyclic antidepressants: Dry mouth, dizziness, constipation, weight gain, problems urinating, blurred vision, sweating, headaches, fatigue, insomnia, rashes, light sensitivity, anxiety, increased heart rate.

SSRIs (selective serotonin reuptake inhibitors): Loss of interest in sex, difficulty having an orgasm, nausea, upset stomach, constipation, diarrhoea, fatigue, sweating, insomnia, nervousness.

MAO (monoamine oxidase) inhibitors: Dizziness, headaches, mania, confusion, memory loss, insomnia, weakness, sweating, delayed orgasm, fatigue, upset stomach, nausea, constipation, diarrhoea, weight gain, problems urinating, rashes, tremors, increased heart rate.

Serotonin antagonists and reuptake inhibitors: Dizziness, headaches, dry mouth, upset stomach, nausea, constipation, blurred vision, fatigue, sleepiness, anxiety, confusion.

* Not all of the side effects apply to all of the antidepressants in each category. The table is intended as a guide only. Rare side effects are not included, nor are lesser-used types of antidepressants. You should discuss possible side effects with your doctor and read the instructions accompanying an antidepressant very carefully.

Pregnancy and antidepressants

If you're depressed and pregnant then please try not to worry. Your doctor will be doing everything to make sure your condition in no way harms your baby either now or after the birth.

If you're still motivated, if you're sleeping well, if you're eating well and if you're not drinking or taking drugs then there's no need to believe your depression is having any significant effect on your foetus. However, if you can't take care of yourself and aren't sleeping and eating properly then antidepressants may have to be considered in the best interests of yourself and your baby.

Many specialists say that if you were taking

antidepressants for major depression at the time you became pregnant then you should continue to take them. On the other hand, many women have successfully come off antidepressants during pregnancy so there are no hard and fast rules. Let the doctor decide.

If you're depressed and would like to be pregnant but are not pregnant at the moment then you should wait until you've been successfully treated. It will be much better for you and much better for your baby. The only exception might be if your depression is actually to do with being childless.

The use of antidepressants during pregnancy has been linked with short-term problems such as premature birth, lower birth weight, jitteriness and respiratory problems in infancy. There is also some evidence of babies experiencing withdrawal symptoms when their mothers have been taking certain antidepressants. So it's an issue that has to be treated very seriously.

If your depression continues after the birth, or begins after the birth, your doctor still has some weighing up to do because antidepressants will be present in your breast milk.

If your depression can be managed with psychotherapy, combined with support and other practical measures, then that's obviously the safest thing to do. Discuss your concerns with your doctor and let him or her decide what's best.

Antidepressants and your sex life

Many people would be dismayed at any reduction in their sexual capacity and for anyone already suffering from depression the sexual side effects of some antidepressants, especially SSRIs, can be another serious blow. About 40 per cent of men and women report antidepressant-induced sexual dysfunction (ASD). If you find you're losing interest in sex, or that you have difficulty reaching orgasm, that could be due to the effects of antidepressants.

However, depression itself can also cause a loss of interest in sex, so there's the need to strike a balance. If you're sure your sexual difficulties didn't begin until after taking antidepressants then discuss the situation frankly with your doctor. It may be possible to change to a different antidepressant that won't have such an effect.

Q: Is there anything I can do to reverse the impact of SSRIs on my sex life?

A: A doctor at the University of California tested Gingko biloba on patients who were being treated with SSRIs and concluded that it could completely counter their negative effects. No significant side effects were reported over a two-year period. When the Gingko biloba was discontinued, sexual dysfunction returned. So it seems that this could be worth trying, but discuss the issue with your doctor first. You can buy Gingko biloba from health shops.

MYTH: Antidepressants are addictive.

FACT: Antidepressants are not addictive in the true sense of the word. In fact, a big problem in the treatment of depression is patients forgetting to take their antidepressants or deciding to give them up before they should. There could be no clearer evidence that antidepressants are not addictive in the short term. With all antidepressants you might suffer withdrawal symptoms when your treatment comes to an end, but those are usually quite manageable. In some cases, the longer you take antidepressants the longer it takes to come off them. (*To learn more about giving up antidepressants, see Part 3, Chapter 8.*)

Interactions between antidepressants and other things

Antidepressants may interact with other drugs including caffeine and alcohol and even, in certain cases, with foods such as cheese, smoked fish and yeast extracts. In some cases, these interactions can be serious so discuss them with your doctor and read the antidepressant information leaflet extremely carefully.

MYTH: If you take antidepressants you won't be yourself.

FACT: The reality is that depression is robbing you of your true personality. You'll be more yourself with an effective antidepressant. Very, very few patients report such side effects as feeling high or 'strange'.

Q: Do I have to see a doctor if I want antidepressants?

A: Only properly qualified people can prescribe antidepressants. Never take antidepressants bought on the internet or borrowed from friends who have some left over. (*If you want to know about the 'natural antidepressant' St John's Wort, see Chapter 5.*)

4

Psychotherapy

Even if you're taking antidepressants, some form of psychotherapy should ideally be part of your treatment. One of the reasons for this is that psychotherapy can not only cure your depression but, far more effectively than antidepressants, *it can also stop it recurring*. Psychotherapy can also be used on its own.

There's a very important difference between antidepressants and psychotherapy that you need to understand. It doesn't matter which doctor prescribes for you, say, 20 milligrams of Prozac – the effect will always be the same. But it does matter very much which psychotherapist you see. Six psychotherapists may have identical training but each one will adapt things in accordance with his or her own personality. Apart from which, you just may not hit it off with one psychotherapist while you get on like a house on fire with another. In other words:

- Don't give up on psychotherapy just because the first psychotherapist you see doesn't achieve very much for you.

- Give the first psychotherapist a fair chance and if things don't work out switch psychotherapists rather than stop psychotherapy.

If you find it difficult to tell the first psychotherapist you wish to change then ask a friend to phone up for you.

MYTH: Psychotherapy is a con; you just lie on a couch while someone gets paid a lot of money to listen to you.

FACT: There are various kinds of therapy and it's very unlikely you'll be having the type that involves the couch of popular imagination. The most suitable types of psychotherapy for depression have at least as good a success rate as antidepressants.

Q: Can I get psychotherapy on the National Health Service?

A: If your doctor recommends it then psychotherapy is free on the NHS in the UK, but waiting lists are long in some areas. If for some reason NHS therapy isn't available to you, you may be able to receive therapy through a voluntary organization and helplines may also be beneficial (see Part 5, Chapter 14). You could also consider seeing a therapist privately (see page 96). Some of them offer a sliding scale based on your income.

I've always been a very successful person so I couldn't believe it when this happened to me. I opted for therapy and, fortunately, it's worked okay.

Derek

The different kinds of psychotherapy

There are various kinds of psychotherapy:

Counselling Many general practitioners (GPs) now have counselling skills themselves or have counsellors in their surgeries. However, it's important to understand that in the UK there is no legal requirement for counsellors to have passed any exams or be members of any professional body. Nor does the word 'counselling' imply any particular style of therapy. One counsellor may follow one approach while another counsellor might follow a quite different approach. So, if your GP suggests counselling it's important to find out what style of counselling is being proposed and what qualifications the counsellor has.

Psychoanalysis This is the famous 'couch' therapy associated with Sigmund Freud although, in fact, you may not necessarily lie on a couch at all. Psychoanalysis isn't generally used for depression simply because it takes a very long time. However, there is an accelerated version (see 'Psychodynamic therapy').

> *MYTH: Psychotherapy is like stirring up the leaves at the bottom of a pond and it's a very dangerous thing to do.*
>
> **FACT:** Only the 'analytical' styles of psychotherapy concentrate on the 'leaves' and sometimes that's essential. Most other styles are far more interested in what you can do right now to improve your situation.

Psychodynamic therapy This derives from psychoanalysis, sharing the belief that depression and other mental problems may be due to painful feelings held in the unconscious (or subconscious) mind. The main difference to psychoanalysis is that psychodynamic therapy normally targets a specific problem (such as depression) and can therefore be much shorter. Typically, 20 sessions are enough (but you could need as few as eight or, at the other end of the scale, this therapy could go on for years).

Cognitive analytic therapy (CAT) This is a sort of hybrid of psychodynamic therapy (above) and cognitive therapy, which we'll learn more about on page 94.

Gestalt therapy This style of therapy is to do with 'letting it all out' and could be useful for anyone who is highly inhibited.

MYTH: Psychotherapists are usually so mad themselves they couldn't possibly help anybody.

FACT: It's true that some psychotherapists have previously had problems of their own which gave them their interest in the subject but, if anything, that makes them all the better at understanding other people's problems.

Person-centred therapy The key to this approach is that the therapist will accept you and respect you exactly as you are. If you have a lot of doubts about yourself and if you're worried about thoughts and feelings that you have, then this could be the ideal therapy for you.

Interpersonal therapy Relationship problems are a very common cause of depression. The aim of this therapy is to help you deal more effectively with relationships and, at the same time, get away from the idea that your self-worth is entirely dependent on the love and approval you get from others.

Relationship counselling Relationship counselling is very similar to interpersonal therapy but whereas the latter is often aimed at an individual

> **Q:** *How long should I give it before deciding to change therapists?*
>
> **A:** About six weeks should be enough to see if you're getting anywhere, but discuss it with your therapist and your doctor first. It can happen, for example, that no apparent progress is made for several weeks and then, bingo, one day everything begins falling into place.

this style of counselling is for couples or, indeed, families. It's not directly aimed at tackling depression, of course, but relationship problems are often the trigger for depression.

Behaviour therapy If your depression stems, for example, from a deep fear of doing something others consider normal, then this therapy can be a godsend. Effectively, you have a phobia. It's treated in a highly practical way that normally gets very quick results. The therapist will help you, one small step at a time, to do the thing you're afraid of.

Coaching This has really caught on in the past few years, partly because anybody can set themselves up as a coach. You need to be very careful, therefore, before going to see a coach for something as important and complicated as depression. That having said, coaching can be very effective if you're 'fed up' rather than seriously depressed. If the concept appeals to you, try to find a coach who is also a qualified psychotherapist.

Cognitive therapy (CT)/Cognitive behavioural therapy (CBT) These two therapies effectively amount to the same thing, which is that it's our thoughts that always govern our moods (a cognition is simply a more impressive-sounding word for a thought). Positive thoughts tend to make you feel optimistic, confident and happy. Negative thoughts tend to make you pessimistic, nervous and depressed. CT teaches, for example, that other peole can't make you angry. If you get angry that's because you *choose* to be angry. Faced with the same circumstances you could equally *choose* not to be angry.

Some GPs now supply CT materials including CD ROMs for use at home. Your GP may also be able to arrange access to a computerized CBT programme called *Beating The Blues*. It's been recommended by the National Institute for Health and Clinical Excellence (NICE) and has proven highly effective.

Rational emotive behaviour therapy (REBT)
Developed in the 1950s, REBT covers some of the same territory as CT, believing that mental ill health is often caused by irrational thinking.

Hypnotherapy Hypnosis makes you more open to new ideas and more responsive to suggestions, so it can be an excellent way of magnifying the power of psychotherapy. Discuss the matter with your doctor before proceeding.

Q: Which type of psychotherapy is best?

A: It's hard to say for sure because some types have been extensively researched and others hardly at all. If there's reason to believe your depression stems from traumatic events in your past then psychodynamic therapy is indicated. If it's more to do with things in the present then cognitive therapy could be appropriate. The best thing is to find a psychotherapist who is willing and able to take a flexible approach.

Q: If there's a long waiting list for NHS psychotherapy is there anything else I can do?

A: You could go privately (see below). (*For self-help therapies, see Chapter 5*).

Seeing a private psychotherapist

You shouldn't really have to pay for the treatment of depression by psychotherapy in the UK, because it is available on the NHS. However, if there's a long NHS waiting list in your area and if you can afford it you may consider private treatment.

You'll probably go once a week or once a fortnight and, with luck, your treatment might be successful in as few as, say, ten sessions. But, of course, you'll also have to be prepared for it to take longer, so this requires very careful thought. Some counsellors will reduce their fees for clients who would suffer financial hardship. Otherwise use self-therapy and *Beating The Blues* if available to you (see 'Cognitive therapy', page 94) until you reach the head of the queue with the NHS.

Once you have your shortlist get in touch with each of the psychotherapists, outline your problems and ask the following questions. You may prefer to do this by email. If you don't have the energy ask someone to handle it all for you:

- What type or types of psychotherapy do you offer?

- What qualifications do you have?

- How many years have you been a counsellor?

- Do you have experience of dealing with depression?

- How much do sessions cost?

- What frequency would you recommend?

- What happens if I can't come to a session?

- How many sessions do you think would be necessary?

Of course, add any other questions you wish. Even if you make your initial enquiries by email or letter, don't make a decision without speaking to the psychotherapist on the phone or face to face. It's important you feel comfortable.

Q: What's the best way of finding a private psychotherapist?

A: Ask your GP to recommend someone. Contact one of the professional associations and ask for the contact details of local counsellors. Look under 'Counsellors' and 'Psychotherapists' in the Yellow Pages. Ask for recommendations from friends. Then compile a shortlist and follow the advice below. (*To find details of professional associations, contact the British Association for Counselling and Psychotherapy – details in Part 5.*)

What is it like going to a psychotherapist?

If you've made an appointment to see a psychotherapist that's already a very positive sign. It means you've admitted to yourself that there's something wrong. By doing that you've taken an important step forward.

There's absolutely no need to feel apprehensive. Your psychotherapist is just a normal person like you but with special training. You certainly won't be judged or criticized. Think of psychotherapy as going to see a friend for a really good heart to heart, but a friend with considerable insight and wisdom.

Whatever style of therapy you're having, no one can force you to talk about things you don't want to talk about. But, of course, the more frank and open you are the more quickly progress can be made. Try not to be resistant. If you are it may be due to some sort of personality clash with the therapist. If that seems to be the case you may need to consider finding a different therapist.

Every session will be slightly different but, hopefully, they'll always be stimulating and interesting. Sometimes you'll be positive and sometimes you'll be rattled and want to give up.

On the good days you'll feel you've gained an insight and as those accumulate so you'll begin to feel clearer and more optimistic.

Which is best, antidepressants or therapy?

Antidepressants and psychotherapy both have more or less the same level of success, but keep in mind that therapy has fewer side effects than antidepressants (but it can have some). If you do begin with psychotherapy, then if you've not experienced any improvement after six to eight weeks, your doctor may suggest adding antidepressants to the treatment.

In fact, there's no reason why you can't take antidepressants *and* see a psychotherapist *and* practise the self-help techniques in the next chapter. The more things you do the more quickly you're likely to get better.

Other treatments available through your doctor

If neither antidepressants nor psychotherapy works, or if your doctor has particular reasons for suspecting something unusual, there are other possible lines of treatment. For example, there is evidence that some cases of depression are due to a virus. Another avenue to explore is that of food allergies and undiagnosed coeliac disease.

Treatment is getting better all the time. So if your depression has so far proven resistant to conventional methods please don't despair.

5

Self-help and alternative treatments

There are several immediate steps you can take to help yourself when you're suffering from depression. That doesn't mean, of course, that you're in any way to blame for your illness it's just that, as with many other illnesses, there are things you can do to aid your recovery. In fact, where depression is concerned you should *always* try to do things to help yourself as much as possible. You'll get better faster. So even if you're taking antidepressants and even if you're seeing a psychotherapist you should *still* follow as many of the self-help treatments in this chapter as you can.

By the way, in America they call self-help treatment from books 'bibliotherapy'. They take it very seriously. Don't just stick with this book, in Part 5, Chapter 16 you'll find details of other books it would also be helpful to read.

Setting goals for recovery

The first thing you need to do is set some goals because recovery from depression is usually a step-by-step process. It's therefore very important for your confidence that you take note of each of those steps and celebrate them.

Obviously the goals you set will be dependent on your own personality and the severity of the problems you're facing now. Part of a set of goals might look like this, for example:

- I will tackle one of the tasks I've been putting off.

- I will go to work.

- I will go out for a meal with my partner/ family/friends.

- I will watch a funny film and laugh.

As you reach each of these goals, so you should give yourself some sort of reward both to celebrate the occasion and to give yourself something extra to look forward to.

Foods that fight depression

The idea of eating yourself better sounds too good to be true, doesn't it! And yet various experiments have shown that in *certain* cases dietary changes alone can overcome depression.

The three-prong approach

Many nutritionists believe you should follow the three-prong approach to help combat depression. However, it has to be stressed that if you're not deficient then extra quantities probably won't be of any benefit.

Prong 1

It's suggested that you consume plenty of:

• Complex carbohydrates.

• Folic acid (folate).

• Omega-3.

• Selenium.

> *Q: What are Omega-3 oils?*
>
> **A:** Omega-3 is simply a type of fat that has various benefits, including keeping the blood more mobile and arteries more flexible.

Prong 2

It's suggested that you should try to cut down on:

- Food additives.

- Alcohol.

- Recreational drugs.

Prong 3

Ask your doctor to consider testing you for food allergies, especially to wheat, milk and corn.

A full explanation of the three-prong plan is given next.

REMINDER

Serotonin is one of the chemicals in the brain which is responsible for sending 'happy' messages.

Prong 1 – Foods it may be helpful to eat

Complex carbohydrates As you now know, low serotonin is thought by many scientists to be linked to depression. There is a natural way of helping your body to boost serotonin and that's to eat plenty of carbohydrates. Choose the so-called complex carbohydrates such as pasta, vegetables, cereals and bread because they release energy steadily.

Folic acid (folate) Raw green leafy vegetables such as spinach (together with yeast extracts, nuts, whole grains and liver) contain large quantities of folic acid (folate). Deficiency has been linked by some scientists with depression and also with dementia and schizophrenia.

Omega-3 Depression has been linked by some specialists with low levels of a polyunsaturated fatty acid (PUFA) known as Omega-3. Omega-3 is principally found in oily fish, especially mackerel, herring, salmon and tuna. Note that if you're pregnant

---

Q: What can I do if I don't like greens?

A: You might like to consider taking a supplement of about 400 micrograms of folic acid (available in health food shops).

some experts say you shouldn't eat swordfish, shark or fresh tuna more than once a month and shouldn't eat fish from inland waters at all. If you are vegetarian or vegan, or just want to avoid fish, a good non-fish source of Omega-3 is flaxseed oil (also known as linseed oil), available in health food shops. Other non-fish sources are rape seed oil, soya, walnut oil and walnuts.

Selenium According to some scientists, a low intake of the trace mineral selenium correlates with anxiety, fatigue and depression. One way of ensuring you have enough selenium is to eat a couple of freshly shelled Brazil nuts every day (but not more than six because selenium is toxic in high doses). Alternatively you might like to consider taking a supplement.

MYTH: Brazil nuts can cause cancer.

FACT: It's not the Brazil nuts but a toxin (aflatoxin) formed by certain moulds that can grow on Brazil nuts and, come to that, other nuts too. To be safe, the European Union strictly controls the import of Brazil nuts. As a precaution, eat only nuts that are ivory white inside.

Prong 2 – Things you might like to avoid

Food additives So far only a few additives have been directly linked with depression but it makes sense, as a precaution during this very difficult time, to try to cut down on food additives as much as possible.

MYTH: When you lead a busy life there just isn't time to prepare meals without convenience foods that have additives.

FACT: It certainly isn't easy. However, you might be surprised how quickly fresh produce can be prepared and cooked. For example, you can prepare a wholesome meal of fresh steamed or stir-fry vegetables in less than 30 minutes. Of course, convenience foods are fine occasionally but it's best not to make them your regular meals.

> *Q: What can I use to sweeten my food and drinks if I'm slimming and want to avoid additives?*
>
> **A:** Quite honestly, you'll be doing yourself a favour if you get used to food and drinks without sweetening them. Within a couple of days your taste buds will adjust and you'll hardly notice the difference. If you want to use an artificial sweetener ask your pharmacist to recommend one.

Alcohol Most people would associate alcohol with having a good time. However, according to the Royal College of Psychiatrists, regular heavy drinking can actually cause depression. In addition, high alcohol consumption can lead to:

- Dementia (memory loss).
- Psychosis (delusions).
- Alcohol dependence.
- Suicide.
- Poor performance at work.
- Family arguments.
- Sexual problems.

What's more, even relatively small amounts of alcohol can lead to panic attacks in susceptible individuals. What happens is that as the alcohol wears off, you suffer withdrawal symptoms that feel like, and therefore cause, anxiety.

Alcohol, then, is not a way of relieving anxiety or depression but something that will actually make the situation worse. The easiest way to keep a check on your drinking is to count the number of 'units'.

One unit of alcohol is equivalent to:

• A standard pub measure of spirits.

• A small glass of wine.

• A half pint of *normal* strength beer or lager.

So how many units can you safely drink? The UK Department of Health guideline states that men should drink no more than three to four units in any one day or 21 units per week, and that women should drink no more than two to three units in any one day or 14 units per week.

Women have a lower limit than men because, on average, they weigh less.

Self-test

Do you:

❏ Use alcohol as a way of coping with feelings of frustration, anxiety or depression?

❏ Use alcohol to give you more confidence?

❏ Often have hangovers – you feel shaky and anxious when you wake up?

❏ Row with people after drinking?

❏ Become gloomy or aggressive after drinking?

❏ Feel suicidal after drinking?

❏ Need more alcohol than you used to in order to feel good?

❏ Start drinking earlier and earlier in the day?

If you answered 'yes' to any of those questions then please be aware that you could be heading for a problem with alcohol. Keep an eye on things. If you answered 'yes' to most or all of the questions, please try to cut down or even to stop drinking altogether. In today's culture it's very easy to lose sight of the fact that alcohol is potentially very harmful.

Also bear in mind that a unit is only a very rough way of assessing your alcohol intake. One pint of extra strong beer (8–9 per cent proof) is equivalent to four and a half units, for example – so that's more than the safe daily limit.

Cutting down on alcohol

It may be that you're one of those rare people who can simply cut down to the target amount or even give up straight away. However, going 'cold turkey' can often lead to withdrawal symptoms that many people find intolerable. If that's the case then you'll be more likely to succeed if you cut down gradually. If you go to the pub with friends, drink half pints instead of pints, for example.

Step 1 Work out exactly how much you do drink in a week by making a note of every drink you have each day and at the end of a week total it all up – you may well be surprised.

Step 2 Set realistic targets for reducing your alcohol consumption week by week.

Step 3 Find alternative things to do other than drink and keep away from the sort of situations in which you normally feel very tempted to drink. Try to enlist the help of your partner; if your partner also drinks heavily encourage him or her to join you.

Bear in mind that, initially, you may feel worse when you stop drinking. This is due to withdrawal symptoms and it's going to make it all the harder. However, try to keep in mind that they won't last long and if your depression is alcohol-related that, too, will be gone in about a month. Nonetheless, if you have been drinking consistently large amounts of alcohol for many weeks or months and think you may have a problem with alcoholism or alcohol dependence, then do not suddenly stop drinking altogether because there is a risk that you may suffer fits. Consult your doctor first.

You may well find that your depression goes away without any other treatment once you stop drinking. (*To get outside help to cut down on alcohol, see Part 5, Chapters 14 and 15.*)

MYTH: Real men drink a lot.

FACT: On the contrary, men who do dangerous jobs or take part in high-risk sports and activities drink very little. It just isn't possible to function at the highest level under the influence of alcohol.

MYTH: Alcohol makes you more sexy.

FACT: Alcohol reduces inhibitions and that can help you to enjoy sex more. But physical response is actually impaired by alcohol in both women and men. The real solution is to learn to be less inhibited without alcohol.

Prong 3 – Check for food allergies with your doctor

It's quite possible your depression could be caused by a food allergy, especially if your symptoms include chronic fatigue. It would be wise to discuss the possibility of food allergies with your doctor. The three most common foods that cause the condition are **wheat**, **milk** and **corn**. However, many others might be implicated as well.

As a little girl I was diagnosed with coeliac disease and put on a gluten-free diet, which I hated because it made me feel different from my friends. So you can imagine how happy I was when the symptoms disappeared in my early teens. Soon I'd forgotten all about it. Then I became depressed. Over several years I was given every kind of treatment but nothing helped. Fortunately, a new doctor spotted the coeliac connection. I went back on the gluten-free diet and within a few weeks I was completely better. It was like a miracle.

Isabel

Coffee – the good and the bad

Coffee turns out to be something of a double-edged sword where depression is concerned. Coffee can overcome mild depression, but it can also cause anxiety and panic attacks. The substance that gives coffee its kick is, of course, caffeine, which is also in tea and some soft drinks. So how can you know whether to give up coffee or to drink more of it?

- If you don't have coffee or other drinks containing caffeine and you're suffering from mild depression try gradually introducing coffee.

- If you're already drinking one to four cups of coffee a day or equivalent and feeling depressed it's unlikely that coffee has much to do with it. It would be unwise to drink much more. *In one experiment, 25 per cent of people reported panic attacks after being given eight cups of coffee a day.*

- If you're drinking five or more cups of coffee a day or equivalent and suffering nervousness, anxiety, increased heart rate, insomnia or panic attacks it may be that caffeine is the cause. Try giving it up and see what happens.

How to give up caffeine

If you suspect your problems are due to too much caffeine it's best to cut down gradually. Going 'cold turkey' will almost certainly make you feel depressed for about a week and quite probably cause withdrawal-related headaches. An easier way is to cut out one cup of coffee (or other drink containing caffeine) at a time and then give your body two or three days to adjust before cutting out another one.

St John's Wort

St John's Wort (Latin name *Hypericum perforatum*) has been in use for hundreds of years as a remedy for mild depression. However, although it's a 'natural' herbal remedy you shouldn't make the mistake of assuming that it's therefore completely safe. Don't take it without your doctor's approval.

> **Important**
>
> St John's Wort should not be taken if you are pregnant or breastfeeding, and it should not be given to babies or children. St John's Wort can interact with other drugs, particularly prescription antidepressants, birth control pills, Warfarin, Digoxin, Cyclosporine, Irinotecan and Indinavir.

I wouldn't say I was really depressed. I just felt sad all the time. I lay awake a lot at night thinking about problems that, in the daylight, didn't seem like problems at all. So I tried St John's Wort. I can't prove that it worked but over a period of about three months I gradually felt better.

Barbara

The importance of exercise

It could well be that the quickest way for you to tackle depression is by dancing or taking the dog for a walk. That may sound absolutely ridiculous – what, after all, have those things got to do with the way you feel about a sad or worrying event? – and yet it's true. Exercise is one of the treatments recommended for mild depression by the National Institute for Health and Clinical Excellence (NICE). Not only that, several scientific studies have found that exercise is as effective as antidepressants in the treatment of mild to moderate depression and also beneficial to those suffering from severe depression.

Of course, when you're depressed the last thing you feel like doing is going for a run. But maybe you can take Rover for a stroll or put on your favourite music and bop around for a minute or two. Just think about it. Here's a treatment that:

• Doesn't involve taking any pills.

• Doesn't have to cost very much or even anything at all.

• Produces fast results and has a high success rate.

> **MYTH:** *You get enough exercise round the house or at work.*
>
> **FACT:** To be of benefit you need to get your heart rate up into the 'aerobic range' (in practical terms, around 100 to 130 beats a minute, depending on age) and keep it there for a sustained period. Housework just doesn't do that and nor do most jobs.

In fact, your general practitioner (GP) may be able to refer you to an exercise programme. Well over 1,000 GP referral schemes are in place in the UK and the number is growing all the time.

You should be aiming to build up to twenty to thirty minutes of exercise three to five times a week. That may sound like a lot but most people surprise themselves when they discover how quickly they achieve it, usually in two to three months. That's the target level because it can double the level of endorphins in your blood. Endorphins, you may remember, are chemicals that make you feel good.

You don't have to dress up in running shorts or be an athlete or, in fact, follow any particular exercise, you can do whatever you enjoy. Remember, the less fit you are now the more quickly you'll notice your progress. So that's something to look forward to.

Getting the maximum benefit

Not everyone wants to follow an exercise programme and some people can't, but if you're someone who is attracted to the idea you may be interested to know how you can achieve the optimum effect for beating depression. Of course, you're not expected to achieve the target level straight away. You'll need to build up gradually.

What you're actually aiming for is to keep your heart at between 60 and 80 per cent of your maximum heart rate (MHR) for 20 minutes. Your maximum heart rate is:

220 minus your age

In order to monitor your heart rate while exercising you might like to consider buying a heart rate monitor. They're available quite cheaply in sports shops.

MYTH: I just don't have time for exercise.

FACT: And how much time have you got for being depressed? The increased energy you'll have through exercise will more than compensate for the time it takes.

What's the best exercise?

In general, the best form of exercise for depression-busting is:

• Something you can do any time, anywhere without special equipment.

• Something that doesn't need special skills or instruction.

• Something you can do alone or with friends.

• Something you can do all year and that isn't too weather dependent.

• Something you enjoy doing.

• Something that's free.

> **MYTH:** *I'm too overweight to exercise.*
>
> **FACT:** There are still ways of exercising that are likely to be suitable for you, such as swimming and cycling. However, you should consult your doctor first.

Jogging is certainly one of the things that meets nearly all those criteria. As to whether or not you enjoy it, very much depends on you. However, lots of people who stick it out for the first couple of weeks or so do get hooked.

If you're not used to jogging it may be that you almost *can't* jog. Never mind. Just walk as briskly as you can every other day. Gradually build up until you can walk for about half an hour. Once you've reached that level *then* you can start jogging. Just introduce a few seconds of slow jogging into your walk at, say, minute intervals. Build up from there. Your target is to mix walking and slow running over a 30-minute period until you can run non-stop for 20 minutes with a 5-minute walk at the start to warm up and a 5-minute walk at the end to cool down. Remember, we're not talking about sprinting for 20 minutes. We're just talking about keeping moving.

> *MYTH: No pain no gain.*
>
> **FACT:** This catch phrase simply isn't true. In fact, you'll do better exercising at a level at which you can still hold a conversation.

Don't get discouraged if there seems to be a period in which you don't make much progress. Your body has to adjust to the new demands you're making on it and that takes time. Your body will gradually adjust and as it does so the endorphin effect will climb and climb. You'll be amazed.

When I started I couldn't run for more than 20 seconds. At the end of a month I was running on the treadmill for 20 minutes.

Nicola

Keeping motivated

If you can rope somebody else into your exercise programme you can cajole one another along. You may also find it helps if you can exercise in a useful way. For example, maybe you could walk, jog or cycle to work. If it's too far, maybe you could park the car, say, a mile from work (where the parking is cheaper) and jog in from there.

Another way to keep motivated is to set targets – you could do the depression test in Part 1, Chapter 1 every fortnight to see how you're getting on (pages 8–9). You don't need special clothes for a lot of activities but if it helps motivate you then, by all means, buy exercise clothes that make you feel positive about the whole thing.

WARNING

If you're not used to exercise, especially if you're over the age of 40 (35 if you're a smoker), you should consult a doctor before beginning an exercise programme.

Q: Losing weight would make me feel better about myself but will exercise do it?

A: The level of exercise we're talking about here could result in you losing one to two pounds a month, provided you eat the same amount of food. That may not sound a lot but it could amount to a stone or more in a year.

MYTH: I'm too old.

FACT: You're never too old to take some exercise. Noel Johnson ran his first marathon at the age of 72 and went on to run the New York City Marathon at age 92.

MYTH: Women shouldn't exercise because they'll develop ugly muscles.

FACT: Whether or not you consider muscles on women ugly or attractive is a matter of personal taste. The truth is that you'd have to do vastly more exercise than we're talking about here in order to develop prominent muscles.

Massage

When you're not able to exercise, massage can produce some of the same physical and psychological benefits. Why not buy a book on massage and practise with your partner or a friend? From time to time you could also go along to a health spa for a truly relaxing professional session – there's almost certainly one near you.

6

Self-therapy

Think positively

Every day most of us have thousands of negative thoughts:

- This looks difficult.

- I don't think I can do this.

- This is going to be a disaster.

But we balance them with thousands of positive thoughts, too. And sometimes we quite deliberately take control of our thoughts to overcome our doubts:

- Other people can do it so it can't be *that* difficult.

- Come *on*! Of course I can do it.

- I'm going to make a success of this.

So how you feel is not just a question of the things that happen to you, it's also a question of the way you react to those things. There's the well-known glass of water. Is it half full or is it half empty?

Here's an example. While trying to park next to you, a man scratches your car. How do you feel? Angry, of course. 'The idiot! Doesn't he know how to drive? Why didn't he take more care? Now my beautiful car is completely ruined. This has spoiled my entire day. In fact, every time I look at my car I'm going to feel sick...' And so on.

Alternatively, you could have thought: 'I've made that kind of mistake myself. I bet he feels really bad about it. I'll tell him not to worry. It's only a tiny scratch. It really doesn't matter.'

In other words, it's not outside events that make you happy or sad but the way you think about them. Now nobody is suggesting you shouldn't have reactions of happiness or sadness and so on. That's normal, and it's what makes us human. You would *want* to feel sad if something tragic occurred. What you don't want to be is trapped in a depression you just can't shake off and that's what can happen. Instead of feeling sad and hopeless about one thing you end up feeling sad and hopeless about *everything*.

Nor is it true that depression only follows really traumatic events. Quite small things can trigger depression. It could be an unkind word, a row with a friend or a tiny mistake at work. One negative thought leads to several and then to hundreds. So it's vital to:

- Ignore your own self-destructive thoughts.

- Shout the destructive thoughts down out loud, if necessary: 'I refuse to listen to you.'

- Take a break. Sometimes the only way to escape those self-destructive thoughts is to take a break from the circumstances that give rise to them. A few hours off, a long weekend or a complete holiday can work wonders.

On the next few pages are some examples of the kind of negative thinking that could lead you into depression, compared with a more positive way of looking at the same kinds of situations. By the way, the idea of positive thinking is endorsed by the National Institute for Health and Clinical Excellence (NICE).

Black and white

This very common way of looking at things leads you to see everything in the same terms as an old-fashioned cowboy movie. Everyone and everything is either 100 per cent 'goodie' or utterly 'baddie', and since almost nothing and no one is completely 'goodie' you tend to see the world in very black terms indeed, including yourself. Similarly, anything less than perfection becomes a failure.

✗ Negative style of thinking:

- Striving for perfection is obviously the right thing to do.

- Not coming first means I'm a failure.

✔ Correct style of thinking:

- I'm really enjoying myself even if my style is far from perfect.

- I'd like to be first but it's hardly a catastrophe if I'm not.

> **MYTH:** *If something is worth doing it's worth doing well.*
>
> **FACT:** On the contrary, if something is worth doing it's worth doing *badly*. What's important is that the thing is *worth* doing. In which case, it would be tragic if you didn't do it at all just because you can't do it perfectly or well.

I'd been brought up on 'only first counts' and I totally believed it. When I was told it was wrong I was, like, 'Are you crazy?' It just seemed obvious. But the more I thought about it the more I realized how I'd been conned all those years.

Shane

> **MYTH:** *The great men and women are perfect and never make mistakes.*
>
> **FACT:** Nobody is perfect and everybody makes mistakes. Winston Churchill is generally considered to have been one of the greatest British statesmen of all time, but even his most fervent admirers point to numerous misjudgements. And the same applies to everyone.

The sweeping generalization

In this style of thinking you extrapolate a whole series of negatives from just one, probably quite tiny little thing, that goes wrong. For example, your handbag gets stolen; or a request gets turned down; or your partner just once points out something you haven't done correctly and you then think as follows:

✗ **Negative style of thinking:**

- Having my handbag stolen just shows how awful people are.

- Every time I do something my partner finds fault with me.

- I'm a failure.

✔ **Correct style of thinking:**

- I've never had anything stolen before, which just shows how honest most people are.

- I've made quite a few mistakes about which my partner never actually said a word.

- I'm a unique individual with strengths and weaknesses.

Jumping to negative conclusions

You assume you know what other people are thinking and it's always negative. For example, you see some friends in a little huddle in a corner, keeping their voices down; or your partner is away on a business trip and doesn't ring at the time you expected. You then have the following thoughts:

✗ Negative style of thinking:

- Obviously they're saying bad things about me and don't want me to hear.

- Looks like my partner has begun an affair with someone at work.

✔ Correct style of thinking:

- It seems they're having an interesting discussion; I'll join them.

- Looks like my partner is getting plenty of business.

Mountains out of molehills

This well-known phrase captures this style of thinking perfectly. Your boss criticizes your work; or the bubbly at your wedding doesn't taste very nice. Then you think like this:

✘ Negative style of thinking:

- Obviously I'm going to get the sack.

- I've been planning this for months and now the whole thing is ruined.

✔ Correct style of thinking:

- This problem is tiny and I can put it right very easily.

- I'm thrilled about the whole thing and this is utterly insignificant.

I feel it, therefore it's true

This is a slightly difficult concept but it works like this. On the emotional level you have a certain reaction to something or feel a certain way and, as a result, believe that your emotion reflects the reality. For example, you walk into a party where people are dancing and no one takes any notice of you; or a huge man in a pub insults you and challenges you to a fight. Then you think like this:

✗ Negative style of thinking:

- No one takes notice of me because I'm insignificant.

- I'm a coward otherwise I wouldn't have been frightened.

✔ Correct style of thinking:

- I'm as significant as everybody else; they're just very busy.

- Boxers aren't allowed to fight men much bigger than themselves and nor will I.

Wrongly taking personal responsibility

Taking personal responsibility is a positive character trait but it becomes distorted when you start to take responsibility for things for which you have no responsibility at all. Let's say your partner gets injured while playing tennis with you, or your elderly father has a driving accident. These are the kinds of responses you have:

✗ Negative style of thinking:

- If I hadn't been hitting the balls so hard this wouldn't have happened. It's all my fault.

- I knew he was too old to drive safely. I should have stopped him. It's all my fault.

✔ Correct style of thinking:

- Other people have to take responsibility for themselves.

Putting yourself down

If you have this outlook you always find a reason to belittle yourself. So you could call it 'molehills out of mountains'. You ignore your successes and the compliments people pay you by telling yourself things like:

✗ Negative style of thinking:

- That was sheer luck.

- Their opinion isn't worth anything.

- I didn't do very much really.

✔ Correct style of thinking:

- That was as a result of my skill.

- I'm very happy other people appreciated what I did.

- I achieved something significant.

Changing to a more positive way of thinking

Did you recognize any of those negative ways of thinking in yourself? Of course you did. Everybody has them to a degree. However, in people who aren't depressed they're balanced by a happy quantity of positive thoughts. If you're depressed, *most* of your thoughts are negative.

So what can you do about it?

A good way of getting started on these negative thoughts is simply to write them down. Buy yourself a large, stiff-backed notebook and enter your thoughts every day.

Hold nothing back, however horrible. If you want to criticize other people then go ahead (do make sure your notebook is put away where other people can't read it). And if you have any positive thoughts include them too.

The mere act of writing is itself a therapy. It can help a lot. Writing things down is also a way of writing them *out*. Put a line right down the middle of the page. Whenever you write something negative put it in the left-hand column. Then see if you can work out any positive view of the same circumstances and put it in the right-hand column. For example, suppose one day you have an argument with your partner and end up feeling he doesn't love you. Then you could set it out like this:

Negative view *28th April* John has just refused to marry me which proves he doesn't love me. I hate him. Anyway, nobody could love me.	Positive view John is living with me and it can't be easy. That must prove that he loves me otherwise he'd go. He only got divorced six months ago so it's under-standable that he's wary of getting married again so quickly.

Of course, when you're depressed it's difficult to imagine any positive thoughts at all. That's what depression is all about. So this isn't going to be easy. But try all the same.

Once you've written a few pages of material, read it through to see if any particular type of negative thoughts are repeated over and over. Some therapists call them automatic negative thoughts (ANTS) because they become habitual. Use a fresh page to set them down and then try to counter them.

Automatic negative thoughts	Counter arguments
I'll never be any good at anything.	There may be things I can't do but there are many other things I can do perfectly well.
I'm too old to be able to enjoy the things I used to.	Hey, what things? I can still talk, eat, read, go to the cinema, walk, swim, make love, feel, look after my grandchildren... The list is endless.

The next stage is to take this a little bit further and see if you can actually identify any negative styles of thinking that aren't really warranted by the facts.

Step 1 Identify your ANTS. Write them down.

Step 2 Analyse these negative thoughts to see if they're really valid. It might be a good idea to get a second opinion from a friend.

Step 3 If they're not valid, see if you can identify where the error of thinking lies.

You could then draw up a table like this:

Negative thought	Valid (yes/no)	Error
It's my fault John failed his interview because I didn't press his suit.	No	Wrongly taking personal responsibility – John could have pressed his own suit.

(*To find out more about self-therapy, see Part 5, Chapter 16 for some books on the subject.*)

Dealing with suicidal thoughts

If you've seriously entertained suicidal thoughts don't keep quiet about them. Please reach out for the help that's there for you from your family and from the professionals. The dedicated staff at the Samaritans are devoted to helping anyone in your situation. Telephone them on: 08457 90 90 90. (*For other helplines, see Part 5, Chapter 14.*)

If you've already made a suicide attempt you probably haven't thought realistically about the impact on those closest to you. You may have been thinking: 'They'll be better off without me' or something like that. You are utterly wrong. Please understand that. No one is going to be better off without you. In fact, they're going to be very, very much worse.

The reality is that the impact of your suicide will be catastrophic and devastating. If you have children their lives will be shattered. They may find it hard to believe you ever loved them. Their self-esteem will be destroyed. If they're young children they may additionally have problems coping with life on a practical level. They'll probably go on to become depressed in their turn. If you have parents they will be grief-stricken, overcome by guilt (no matter that they did everything they could to look after you) and become physically ill; they will possibly die years before they should have done. If you have a partner his or her happiness will be destroyed for a long, long time; possibly years.

Step 1 Sit down somewhere quiet and close your eyes.

Step 2 Call up an image of the person closest to you. Now try to imagine that person discovering your body or hearing the news of your suicide. Envisage the tears, the grief, the pain, the shock...

Step 3 Analyse the effects of your suicide on that person. What will it be like to come home when you're no longer there? What will it be like at meal times? At bed time? On your birthday? At Christmas? How will they cope emotionally? What will the financial situation be? How will they manage the practical things in life without you?

Step 4 Repeat Steps 1 to 3 for everyone you know.

Step 5 Repeat the whole exercise every day.

Light and sleep

Being 'dosed' with bright light is not only beneficial to people suffering from seasonal affective disorder (SAD) but to those suffering from 'ordinary' depression, too.

When you think about it, it's hardly surprising. After a long spell of gloomy weather we all feel our spirits lift as the sun comes out. So the idea that light could reduce the symptoms of depression doesn't seem at all far-fetched. Scientists aren't certain exactly what's going on, but whatever the precise mechanism, the implications are clear. You need to get plenty of sunshine, especially in winter.

- In winter, take a stroll whenever the sun is out – better still, go for a run or take some other form of exercise that you enjoy.

- If you've had your winter's day exercise already, find a sheltered corner to sit and just feel the warmth of the sun on your closed eyelids.

- In summer, do a little sunbathing – the action of sunlight on the skin is also beneficial. (Take proper precautions against sunburn, of course;

it's best to sunbathe for a short while every day *never* getting sunburned.)

SAD lamps

Unfortunately, in Britain the winter days are short and the skies cloudy and it's impossible for some people to get the amount of sunlight they need. If you feel that way you should buy a special SAD lamp and use it regularly. Don't stare directly at the lamp. Just sit close to it while you get on with something such as reading, writing or eating a meal.

Q: What's so special about SAD lamps and why isn't ordinary room light enough?

A: SAD lights contain fluorescent bulbs behind a special diffusing screen. To be therapeutic the light needs to be 5 to 20 times higher than typical illumination in the home or office.

Q: How long should I sit by a SAD lamp?

A: With the more powerful lamps (those rated at 10,000 lux) some people improve in as little as 15 minutes a day but a typical session would last around 30 minutes. With a lamp rated at a quarter of the power (2,500 lux) you'd have to sit there four times longer.

Sleep

There's also evidence that sleeping too much could be linked to depression. There's a lot of research going on but as yet related treatments are experimental. Obviously there could be a link with the amount of light you receive each day, or it could be something else. Many experts say you should never spend more than eight hours a day in bed.

Yoga

Yoga is an excellent way of reducing stress, anxiety, fatigue and depression while, at the same time, increasing energy and a sense of well-being.

Don't go thinking that yoga isn't for you. Yoga is for everybody irrespective of age, sex, weight, shape or degree of physical fitness. What's more, although it has a spiritual side yoga isn't a religion so it doesn't matter what religion you follow or even if you're an atheist. You may also find it very helpful to delve into the philosophical aspects of yoga. The word means 'union'. Yoga means you no longer feel separated or isolated. You are no longer alone.

Meditation

Meditation can help you beat depression. It could make you:

- More calm.

- Better able to block the negative thoughts that are related to depression.

Rather than explain what meditation is, it might be clearer to describe its *opposite*. The opposite of meditation is having dozens of different thoughts running through your mind every minute and then worrying about them, analysing them and trying to work out what to do. In other words, being normal. The aim of meditation, by contrast, is to empty your mind of all extraneous thoughts so you feel calm.

Step 1 – Sit comfortably You've probably seen photographs of people meditating in the lotus position with their feet on their thighs. That certainly isn't essential. You can simply sit on the floor with your legs crossed. Alternatively you can sit in a chair but make sure you sit upright with your back away from the back of the seat and your feet on the floor. Let your hands drop onto your thighs close to your knees with your fingers curling over your knees. You can also lie down but make sure you don't fall asleep.

Step 2 – Focus Close your eyes and focus on your breathing. Concentrate on your belly expanding for a count of seven as your breathe in. When you breathe out your belly should contract for a count of 11. Smile.

Step 3 – Continue for 5 minutes initially, working up to 15 minutes Some people like to set an alarm clock. While others find they can guess the time fairly accurately. See what works for you.

Q: Why bother to meditate when I already spend several hours asleep every day?

A: The meditative state is quite different from the sleeping state involving different brain wave patterns.

Q: *When should I meditate?*

A: Some people like to meditate as soon as they wake up. Others prefer the evening, to wind down after the pressures of the day. Of course, you can do both.

Meditation made me feel better able to cope and although it takes half an hour every day I seem to have more time than I used to.

Naheed

Q: *How can I stop the thoughts that just keep coming into my mind?*

A: The important thing is not to pursue the thoughts. Just let them come and go if they must. Return to concentrating on your breathing or your candle or whatever it is you're using. As you get better at it you'll be less and less bothered by these thoughts.

Take courage

The self-help and alternative therapies described in Chapters 5 and 6 are all worth trying. But don't expect to get better after just a few days. Certainly don't give up because you're not cured in a week or two. Persist with them. With the exception of St John's Wort they are all things you can and should continue to practise throughout your life. In Part 3 of the book we'll be looking at strategies for living with depression, rebuilding your life after depression and, hopefully, remaining free of it for the rest of your life.

7

Learning more about depression

Depression can be truly terrible. When things are at their very worst there's almost nothing sufferers won't do, including self-harming in the hope of somehow transforming emotional pain into physical pain. If you're depressed you feel utterly worthless, a burden to others and that you could never, ever be happy again. Fortunately, it's now known that severe depression is an illness. An illness that can be cured.

So make a little time to read this chapter and understand all about depression and its causes. For those living with someone with depression, this chapter should give you a clearer picture of this horrible illness and an understanding of why sufferers just can't simply 'snap out of it'.

Someone who has never been depressed – depressed in the medical sense, that is – can probably never fully understand how it feels. Although depression does seem to incorporate the feelings of sadness, futility, worthlessness, incomprehension and, often, anger that we all get from time to time, the experience of it is actually something very different.

What is depression?

Professor Lewis Wolpert, the well-known embryologist, admits in his book *Malignant Sadness* that he, too, had once been a believer in snapping out of it or what he called the 'Sock School of Psychiatry – just pull them up when feeling low.' But when he was struck by serious depression himself he learned that pulling socks just didn't work. 'There were days,' he wrote, 'when I could barely get up.'

Think about it. Here we have an intelligent and highly motivated man, known and respected around the globe, admitting that despite his own scientific training, he couldn't beat depression without professional help. How much less likely it is for those of us without a medical background to be able to beat depression alone! Professor Wolpert's book is very useful and you'll find the details in Part 5, Chapter 16.

Professor Wolpert wasn't ashamed to admit to depression, despite his considerable reputation, and you shouldn't be either.

Admitting the problem is part of the cure.

Depression is one of those unfortunate words that doesn't have a very clear meaning. When you're a bit fed up, when you've got the blues, when you're sad about something that's happened you may say you're 'feeling depressed'. Equally, when you're lying in bed unable to summon the energy to get up, full of a pain that feels as much physical as mental, and thinking constantly of suicide you may also say you're 'feeling depressed'. Two words and two very different meanings.

It's important to make clear that people who are fed up and sad are just as deserving of help as those with clinical depression. However, it would be helpful to have another word for 'serious depression'. We've all been depressed in the everyday sense of the word and it tends to make us think that those diagnosed with depression are just sort of wallowing in sadness and low spirits when they should be 'pulling themselves together'. Well, in fact, there *are* different words but, unfortunately, they sound so scientific and scary no one would use them in everyday conversation. Nevertheless, as you may come across them when discussing your situation with health care professionals, they're explained below.

Different kinds of depression

Some of the words used by professionals can sound rather alarming, but they're not really, it's just the way health professionals talk between themselves.

Endogenous Having its origin *within* the body. In other words, depression caused by a physical problem; possibly with a genetic (that is, inherited) element.

Exogenous (also called **Reactive**) Having its origin *outside* the body. In other words, triggered by external problems such as bereavement or financial worries.

Dysthymia Depression that is chronic (long-lasting) but not generally severe enough to be termed 'clinical depression'.

Cyclothymia Where somebody's mood fluctuates up and down more than is usual, but not severely enough to be termed bipolar disorder.

Bipolar disorder Also known as 'manic depression'. An illness in which sufferers oscillate between deep depression and extreme high spirits (mania).

Primary disorder The mood disorder is the main underlying disorder.

Secondary disorder The mood disorder is the result of another underlying disorder (for example, thyroid problems).

Another way of categorizing depression is in terms of severity. Doctors use a scale, such as the Hamilton Rating Scale for Depression (HRDS) and total up a patient's scores to determine whether the illness is:

- Mild.

- Moderate.

- Major (clinical).

There is also:

Involutional melancholia A form of depression that comes on slowly around the age of 40–55 in women and 50–65 in men. Symptoms may include anxiety, restlessness, insomnia and even anorexia. There may also be paranoia (delusions and hallucinations).

Postnatal (postpartum) depression (PND) If you've recently given birth and are feeling rather low don't feel guilty about it. It's very common and perfectly understandable given the stresses your body has been through. Up to one in seven new mothers feel so low they experience PND, which is very similar to 'normal' depression. If you feel miserable, tired, irritable, unable to enjoy your baby, unable to cope, and unable to sleep or eat properly even when you have the opportunity then you've got PND. You may also get panic attacks. It can be treated in the same way as normal depression but there are also some practical steps that can be taken. The most important thing is to get help from your partner, your mother, your partner's mother, your sister – *someone* – so that you get time to rest and recover from all the stress. Of course, you should also be seeking help from your doctor and health visitor.

Seasonal affective disorder (SAD) About five per cent of people in high latitudes – women especially – experience SAD in winter. If you feel low in winter but not in summer then SAD could be the reason. One possible explanation of SAD is that the action of sunlight on the eyes releases chemicals that promote a sense of well-being. Without that sunlight in sufficient quantities vulnerable people become depressed.

Chronic fatigue syndrome (CFS) Fatigue is a symptom of depression and it's therefore not unreasonable to suppose that depression and CFS could be linked. Chronic fatigue syndrome causes severe physical and mental fatigue that lasts for at least six months and is not caused by a physical disease. Although some patients suffering from CFS show no signs of depression, the majority do exhibit symptoms of at least moderate depression.

Health anxiety disorder (hypochondria) If you suffer from health anxiety disorder, that is, the persistent fear that you may have a serious illness, it could be that your worries and even physical symptoms are a feature of depression. Research shows that those who have hypochondria are ten times more likely to be depressed than other people.

Those who have experienced both mild depression and major (or clinical) depression report that they feel like completely different things. However, all the evidence suggests that they're not actually different things at all and that major depression is a progression from mild depression. You don't wake up one morning with major depression. Rather, there's a gradual process which takes days or even weeks. This is why it's important to tackle depression early on rather than take the risk of it progressing to major depression.

Logically, the kinds of treatments that work for mild depression should also work for major depression. But, of course, the doses may be different and the time scales may be different as well.

In the last ten years I've broken both legs in a climbing accident, had cancer and suffered from clinical depression. I'd rather break both my legs again or suffer a recurrence of cancer than have to go through another bout of depression. It's an all enveloping, total pain that just can't be described.

Gary

How do you get depression?

If you're suffering from depression then you think in a negative way. Your brain will also contain more 'negative' chemicals than the brain of a happy person. But which comes first? The thoughts or the chemicals?

When it comes to treatment it doesn't really matter. Your doctor could prescribe you 'positive' chemicals, that's to say, antidepressants, and they, in turn, would cause you to develop more positive thoughts. Alternatively, a therapist could teach you how to have more positive thoughts and they, in turn, would cause you to develop more 'positive' chemicals.

In other words, there's a kind of circle. Negative thoughts lead to 'negative' chemicals which lead to negative thoughts which lead to 'negative' chemicals... and so on. You can break into that circle at any point, with either antidepressants *or* psychotherapy. Better still, you can break into it at two points with *both* antidepressants and psychotherapy.

Some doctors say depression is almost always linked to an external problem (exogenous), some say it's mostly due to an internal problem (endogenous) and some say it's a mixture of both.

One of the causes of your depression might be that you have experienced a loss. You are much more likely to become depressed following a long-term problem or a long series of different problems than by a single event. There could also be a biological cause.

> *What's it like being depressed? It's like floating towards a waterfall on an airbed. You don't realize anything's wrong and then, wham, suddenly you're over the edge and you need help to get back up. Fortunately, I had that help.*
>
> **Gina**

But why, in similar tragic circumstances, do some people get depression and others not? Statistically, women are twice as likely to become depressed as men. Some experts say it's because women are more given to self-analysis and self-doubt, as well as being more vulnerable to hormonal factors. No doubt the twin pressures many women face nowadays at work and home also play a part.

However, in both sexes there are always some who are more vulnerable than others due to genetic and/or environmental factors. There's very strong evidence of a genetic link for bipolar disorder (manic depression), for example.

Q: I suffer from depression. Does that mean my children will, too?

A: No it doesn't. However, it does mean they could be at slightly higher risk than children in families where there's no history of depression. But there's a positive way of looking at this. You know the signs to look for and you know what it feels like to be depressed. That makes you an ideal parent for a depressed child or young adult to have.

Is depression becoming more common?

Yes, depression is more common than it used to be and it seems that modern life is very much to blame. There are several possible reasons for this:

The breakdown of traditional family life At one time people never lived more than a few miles from where they were born. Families were extremely important and stuck together physically as well as emotionally. However, in recent years things have changed. People don't stay in their home towns as they used to but move away in pursuit of careers. When there are problems there's no one to help. To take an obvious example, if you're a new mother you obviously need a lot of support, but it's very difficult to get it when your own mother lives 200 miles away and your mother-in-law 300 miles away.

Sedentary lifestyle We evolved as physically active creatures, foraging over miles every day in search of fruit, vegetables, nuts, seeds and game. It may be that our bodies just don't function as they should if we don't get a minimum amount of exercise. Certainly, as you saw in Chapter 5, exercise can be a powerful treatment for depression.

Biophilia The naturalist and Pulitzer Prize-winning author Edward O. Wilson popularized the word biophilia, meaning the bond most of us feel with nature. If you have to live in a flat in a city centre without flowers to smell or dogs to cuddle then, no matter how much you like it, you need to find some way to get a little nature back into your life.

Materialism A relentless diet of advertising makes us feel like failures if we don't have all the latest goods and gadgets and that's backed up by programmes and films featuring the lifestyles of the ultra rich.

Loss of religious belief Religion is obviously less important in Western society than it once was and there is evidence that people who have retained strong religious beliefs are less likely to get depression than non-believers. However, spiritual rather than religious feelings may be just as effective. (*To find out more about the mental health benefits of religion and spirituality, see Part 3, Chapter 9.*)

World events At one time people were only aware of problems in their immediate area. We now have to cope with the daily news of personal tragedies and large-scale catastrophes all over the globe.

Young people and depression

Some people find it hard to believe the sad truth that children can suffer from depression and, in fact, even psychiatrists rejected the notion until relatively recently. Nowadays it's generally believed that children as young as three can suffer from depression. But there seems little reason for a particular cut-off. You should always be alive to the possibility of depression in children at any age.

Unfortunately, it can be very difficult to recognize depression in children. It's not easy to distinguish between what's normal and what's abnormal. So here are some signs to watch out for. No single sign, of course, is evidence of depression on its own, but if one of your children exhibits several signs together, over a period, and if that amounts to a significant change in behaviour, then depression should always be suspected. Err on the side of caution and make a visit to your general practitioner (GP).

MYTH: *Only adults get depressed; if kids say they're depressed they're just putting it on.*

FACT: Children do suffer from depression and their numbers are growing at an alarming rate.

Signs of depression in young people

Age 3–5 Sadness, faraway look, anger, timidity, nightmares and difficulty getting to sleep; physical problems such as headaches, nausea, stomach aches and bed wetting; behavioural problems such as aggression, risk-taking, lethargy, hyperactivity or fear of separation.

Age 6–early teens Moodiness, sadness, apathy, irritability, anger, hostility, loneliness, frustration, losing interest in things that used to be enjoyable.

Adolescence Talking of feeling unloved, worthless, stupid, unattractive or friendless; headaches, insomnia, exhaustion, staying in bed; refusing to go to school; aggression, hostility, promiscuity, stealing, lying; losing interest in things that used to be enjoyable; apathy; preoccupation with the occult, death and suicide.

If you are a young person feeling depressed

Rest assured that there are plenty of places you can turn to for uncritical help (see Part 5, Chapter 14).

In so many ways, life has never been tougher for you. It's become routine to have to cope with parents who are rowing, separating and divorcing; living with just one parent (with all the financial implications of that on top); living with a step-parent you don't get on with; bullying; exams; sexual problems... The list seems endless.

If you're feeling depressed as a result then you're far from alone. If you're at school there's almost certain to be at least one other in your class who is feeling the way you do. So don't feel embarrassed about seeking help. If your parents don't understand, you could begin by speaking to the counsellor at your school or to a teacher. You should also make an appointment to see the doctor.

If you're drinking alcohol to help you cope, or resorting to recreational drugs, please try to stop. Really, they actually make depression *worse* not better.

*I'm 15 and I used to hate myself.
I couldn't stand to see my face in the
mirror. I was like, urrgh, that's horrible.
I didn't like my personality. I didn't like
anything about myself. I felt like there
was a sort of weight pressing me down
wherever I went. I saw the doctor and he
sent me for counselling. Now I can fix
my hair in front of the mirror and stuff
like that. I don't think I'm beautiful or
anything but I know how to make
myself look better.*

Lisa

Older people and depression

If you're 50 or more you probably feel you should
know better than to be depressed – but age makes
very little difference. According to the Royal
College of Psychiatrists, for example, around 15
per cent of those aged over 65 are sufferers. As
we've seen, there's even a special kind of
depression that can come on in late middle-age
and which is known as involutional melancholia.

If you're depressed you're certainly not unusual – and it wouldn't be at all surprising. Older people have to face life's big problems. The deaths of friends, of partners, life alone, health worries and much more. If you have the symptoms of depression shown in Chapter 1 (pages 8–9) don't dismiss them as 'normal' for your age. It isn't normal to be depressed at any age. You're just as entitled to the treatments described in Part 3 as anyone.

My husband died last year after 38 years of marriage. Now I'm all alone. I felt as if there was nothing I could do and nothing to live for. Since receiving treatment for depression I've started dancing classes and made some wonderful new friends. Now I have something to look forward to every week.

Enid

Part 3:
Living with Your Depression –
And After

Hopefully, you're now feeling much better than you were. If not, don't get despondent. Just keep on with everything you're doing. Overcoming depression takes time and the longer you've been depressed the longer the struggle to get back to the way you used to be. The main thing is that you keep moving in the right direction. Depression attacks not only your mind but also every aspect of your life. In this part of the book we'll be looking at how you can maintain as normal a life as possible, how you can go on to rebuild your life after your recovery, and how you can have the best chance of remaining free from depression for always.

8

Keeping your life together

Being depressed changes a lot of things. It impacts on your work, your home life, your social life and your love life. That's what makes depression such an awful thing. It can spoil so much, but there are things you can do to minimize the damage. If you're getting over depression you'll now want to put your life back together. Don't expect it all to happen at once. There will be good days and bad days. You'll have to be prepared for that. Take courage. It can be done. Thousands have done it before you and are now enjoying life once more.

Coming off antidepressants

Although you could be on antidepressants for as little as three months the general rule is that you:

- Continue taking antidepressants for at least six months after you start to feel an improvement.

- Take antidepressants for a total of at least eight months (because that's the average amount of time for depression to go away).

However, the doctor will make a decision based on a number of factors. Quite a lot of doctors favour continuing antidepressants for a year after you feel better, rather than six months. If you have had depression on two or more occasions then your doctor is likely to suggest you continue with antidepressants for at least two years. And in certain circumstances – for example, bipolar disorder/manic depression – it may be decided you should continue with a 'maintenance' dose of antidepressants or mood stabilizers indefinitely.

If it should happen that you have to continue with medication please try not to feel despondent. There's really no reason to. Millions of people have to take medicines of various kinds on a permanent basis for such problems as thyroid deficiency, diabetes, glaucoma and asthma. The list is huge. It doesn't make you any less of a person. Antidepressants are just one more substance that some people need to take. It's no big deal. If you need to take antidepressants on a permanent basis then just do it, forget about it and get on with your life.

When the moment is right you'll almost certainly be told to come off antidepressants *gradually*. There's no need to be anxious because you'll be in control of the pace. It won't be a case of suddenly stopping one day, rather, your doctor will probably tell you to slowly reduce the dose over a significant period of time.

Often, if you've only been on antidepressants for a few months you should be able to taper down in a week or two. If you've been on them for a couple of years then withdrawal might take a month or so. And if you've been on them for a decade or more then you might have to taper down over six months.

During this period if you're finding it difficult to judge the effect, talk to your doctor about the possibility of taking a depression test, along the lines of the self-test in Part 1, Chapter 1 (pages 8–9). The result, when compared with an earlier test or tests, will indicate whether or not you're relapsing.

If you start to feel depressed again on a reduced dose then tell your doctor immediately. Usually the best thing to do is increase the dose again just a little. You should find that your depression goes away. If your doctor agrees, you'll probably keep on the slightly increased dose for a couple of weeks and then, once again, resume the phased reduction. You'll almost certainly find you can wean yourself off the antidepressants in this way. Don't jump to the conclusion that problems during the tapering process mean you're relapsing into depression – they could be due to withdrawal symptoms.

Q: What should I do if I start to feel depressed again while tapering off antidepressants?

A: Discuss the matter with your doctor. It's more likely to be withdrawal symptoms. It will probably be suggested that you slightly increase the dose again until you feel better then, after a week or so, resume the tapering process.

Quite frankly it was a relief when my doctor told me I had bipolar disorder because at least I knew what the problem was. So I have to take something. So what. It's no sweat.

Terry

Q: How will I know if I'm suffering from withdrawal symptoms or a return of the depression?

A: This is always difficult. It could be either. If the symptoms disappear as soon as you increase the dose or go back on the antidepressant then it's probably a problem of withdrawal. If you have new symptoms you never had before (such as flu-like feelings) it's probably withdrawal. However, if you continue to feel bad after two or three attempts at tapering then it's probably a relapse.

Maintaining and rebuilding your career

It's not unknown for people with mild depression to do very well at work. They put in long hours as a way of forgetting about personal problems. However, when you're depressed it's far more common to encounter difficulties at work. It may even be that work problems were the cause of the depression, or perhaps you haven't even been able to go to work for a while.

Whatever your precise situation there's almost certainly some sorting out to be done. Maybe your role at work needs to be changed a little. And if you're just about to go back after a long break for depression then you may be having these kinds of thoughts:

• Will everybody know why I've been away?

• Will I be able to cope with my work or will I get stressed?

If you work for one of the larger companies there's unlikely to be any problem about switching roles. Have a chat with the company doctor, the personnel department or your boss. Understandably, a small company may have less room for manoeuvre.

From your own point of view, and also for the benefit of your employers, try not to talk about depression in a negative sort of way. In other words, don't focus on the things you believe you now *can't* do. On the contrary, depression can be a very positive experience. Almost certainly you'll have a better understanding of yourself as well as a better understanding of other people. So that's a new skill you may be able to bring to your work. Talk to your employer in these sorts of terms: 'I now realize I'd be much better suited to Role B', rather than 'I now realize I can't manage Role A.'

Nevertheless, it may be that you'll have a different perspective on work now. Perhaps it will assume less significance in your life. Perhaps you want more time for other things and can manage with less money. That's absolutely fine. We don't all want to make a career the focal point of our lives. In fact, as people get older, many feel that they want to 'downsize' and have an easier life. That's a perfectly legitimate goal.

As to how much you'll want colleagues to know about your situation only you can decide. However, if you do take the bold step of admitting to depression your courage will be admired and you may find other people coming up to you and revealing that they, too, have suffered in the past.

Whether you decide to continue as you were, to accept less responsibility or to seek out more responsibility it's important to keep away from situations you don't enjoy and which you find stressful. Of course, this may involve having to say 'No' to other people from time to time, and that can be very hard. How can you do it without upsetting people or, for example, risking the sack?

Let's say your boss has asked you to take on additional work you fear might stress you too much. You have to find a way of refusing without causing a confrontation or any bad feeling. There is a classic formula in these kinds of situations in which you:

- Acknowledge the other person's point of view.

- Next put your point of view.

- Finish by suggesting a way forward.

You might begin by saying something like this: 'I'm really pleased you've asked me to do this because I can see it's very important.'

Your next step is to state your position: 'However, given my existing workload I just can't see how I can give it the attention it obviously deserves.' Note the use of the word 'however'. It's less harsh than 'but' which can tend to provoke the response of 'No buts.'

The third step is to put forward some sort of constructive proposal such as: 'Can I suggest that someone else takes over my work on the X Project and then I'll have the time to devote to this new client, which would be very exciting?' Your boss now has the opportunity to take up your suggestion or to put forward an alternative. No offence has been caused.

Get organized

Merely organizing things well can reduce stress enormously. If you don't have a good system in place for prioritizing and processing work then have a think about what you can do. A device as simple as a diary can bring about a big change. Simply write down all the things you have to do each day. Then:

- You'll have fewer things to keep in your head.

- You'll no longer feel anxious about missing tasks or appointments.

- You'll be able to see very clearly when you're taking on too much.

Say goodbye to perfectionism

Perfection isn't possible. So striving for it is bound to cause an enormous amount of stress. It'll be much better for you and everybody else if you aim instead for a standard that is reasonable and appropriate. For example will your boss really be more pleased with one piece of almost perfect work rather than three pieces of perfectly satisfactory work?

Perfectionism can lead to depression. When you fail to live up to the impossibly high standards you're setting for yourself you're bound to feel frustrated, self-critical and diminished. You'll never be good enough for yourself, no matter how good other people think you are. So try to be more realistic. Aim for a good standard but not for perfection.

Learn to get help

If you're the sort of person who finds it difficult to delegate then you may be getting overloaded quite unnecessarily. It may be that you:

- Feel too proud to admit you need help.

- Don't want to burden others.

- Feel awkward telling other people what to do.

- Think you would do a better job yourself.

The secret of successful delegating is:

- Finding the right person to delegate to.

- Giving clear instructions (not orders).

- Letting the other person get on with it.

- Accepting the job may not be done the way you would have done it yourself.

Maintaining and rebuilding your finances

Almost everyone has financial problems from time to time. It's just part of life. Perhaps financial worries were a cause of your depression. Even if they weren't, it's quite possible you have financial difficulties now as a result of your depression. It may be that you've been earning less than usual or that you've been spending more than usual in an effort to cheer yourself up.

Your first step should always be to draw up a budget so you can see exactly how much money you have each month and where it goes. You can then look for economies. If that's not enough you might like to consider debt counselling (see Part 5). An expert will then go through your finances with you and advise on your best course of action.

Chill Out

From time to time we all need to just 'chill out.' When pressures are getting too much for you, when stress is building up, when conflicts are becoming too intense, when your head is buzzing and whirring, STOP. Don't have anything more to do with the situations that are causing problems. Take a few hours off or, even, a day or two if you can possibly manage it. Relax with the things you enjoy. When you return to the fray you'll see everything in its true perspective and respond far more effectively.

Maintaining and rebuilding relationships

When you're depressed it may be that your partner, your children and other members of your family have to make adjustments in their own lives. Over time they'll get used to a whole new lifestyle. When you recover they're going to have to adjust again, so this is going to be a very difficult period for all of you. Good communication skills play a big part in coming through successfully. Don't expect your family to change to one style of living and then back again overnight. A little patience is going to be required all round. Also, if there were any problems in your relationships before you became depressed they have to be put right as soon as possible.

You and your partner

There's no such thing as a 'perfect couple' who match one another exactly in every detail. In all relationships there are differences and you have to find a way of dealing with them. In other words, you have to learn to communicate effectively without attacking one another. The first thing you have to realize is that your partner is going to be subject to a great deal of extra stress as a result of your depression. Obviously, the focus is on you but you also need to be sympathetic and understanding towards your partner's situation:

- Encourage your partner to get breaks away from you, if only for a few hours.

- Encourage your partner to seek out self-help groups for 'carers' and other forms of support.

- Don't be resentful when your partner does these things.

Here are some examples of the *wrong* way to communicate:

✗ Negative ways to communicate

- You and your partner criticize one another by using 'labels'. For example, your partner might not want to spend money on something and you then call him 'mean'. Or you just might not be in the mood for sex and your partner then labels you as 'frigid'.

- One of you tries to steamroller over anything the other says, rather than paying attention to it.

- One of you tries to get your way by sulking or threatening to sulk or by withholding emotional support.

How then should you go about communicating? First of all, unless something has happened that means you have to talk urgently, you should wait for a time that's convenient to you both when there will be no distractions. Certain 'ground rules' should be understood:

✔ **Positive ways to communicate**

- Agree that you won't label one another with tags such as 'mean', 'selfish', 'arrogant' or worse.

- Agree that you will not interrupt one another.

- Agree that you will summarize back whatever the other person has said before going on to make your own points. The reason for this is to make sure you both listen as well as speak.

- Agree that you won't speak in anger.

- Agree that you'll mention good things as well as bad.

So how does this work in practice? Let's say you've decided to sit down together one evening at the dining table. The person who has 'called the meeting' begins. If it's you, you can start by explaining what's upset you.

Identifying the problem Things are already off to a good start, but there's a need to pin down the real cause of the problem. Is it that he doesn't love you any more? Let's hear his reply: 'I'm sorry you've been thinking I don't love you. My real problem is that things are going very badly at work. I didn't want to talk about it because I thought it might worry you.'

Finding a solution jointly Now what's your reply? The wrong reply would be 'I'm sorry things are going badly at work but I told you not to take that lousy job. I want you to give it up.' That's hardly finding a joint solution which is what you need to do. A tool to help you achieve that is:

Laying out all the options Using this additional tool you might have said: 'I'm sorry things are going badly at work. Poor you. Hopefully, things will improve but if they don't let's think of other solutions.'

Strategies for coming up with those solutions

- Break down big problems into a series of smaller problems. In this way problems that seem intimidating at first can become more manageable.

- Tackle those smaller problems step by step.

- Be creative. Use 'lateral' thinking to come up with less obvious ideas so you have various options to choose from.

- If your chosen option doesn't resolve the matter then learn from the situation and try to come up with an even better idea.

- Keep your expectations realistic – your partner is a human being like you.

- Be forgiving.

- Be patient.

- Be clear.

When two people have a relationship they often 'fight' for control. This happens all the more if they aren't really very compatible and want to impose their ideas on one another. One way of trying to achieve that – the completely wrong way – is to destroy the other person's self-confidence. When one partner gets something wrong the other immediately jumps on it with criticism and belittling words. Thus the downward spiral of negative thoughts is set in motion.

This is the complete opposite of what a relationship should be all about. If you feel your partner is always putting you down then try to initiate a discussion about it in the way that's been described above.

- Build one another up, don't knock one another down.

- Always find something to praise.

- Never withhold love as a 'punishment'.

- Never take your relationship for granted.

- Never let a day go by without saying 'I love you'.

- Never let a day go by without doing something nice together.

You, your partner and psychotherapy

If you're having psychotherapy you may find your partner feels threatened. He or she may even discourage you from attending sessions. It's an understandable reaction. Your partner may be worried about:

• Being blamed by the therapist for your condition.

• Being usurped by the therapist as the most important person in your life.

• You forming an attachment to the therapist.

• Your personality being changed.

These are completely understandable, but wrong, reactions. Be open about what happens at your psychotherapy sessions and the subjects that have been dealt with. Your partner will then see there's nothing to fear.

My husband made me feel so stupid. I could never do anything right as far as he was concerned. He criticized the least little thing. I used to be full of confidence but within two years I was almost frightened to go out. We went for counselling. He didn't change but I did. I got my confidence back and I left him. Now I'm happy again.

Saskia

The importance of touch

Touching (appropriately, of course) isn't a small matter: if you aren't receiving enough touch it's almost certainly a factor in your depression. Women are generally much better at touching than men. So, men, remember: don't neglect the hand-holding and the cuddling in your relationship with your partner. Also, if you have children, make sure they get plenty of cuddles as well (see page 204).

What's it all about?

Knowing a little bit about the science may help you understand how vitally important touch truly is. It's as essential as air and water. There are at least two lots of chemicals involved: endorphins and oxytocin.

Q: What is oxytocin?

A: Oxytocin is a highly beneficial hormone that increases in response to touch. When someone you like touches you your endorphin level goes up. You feel pleasure. You feel alive. You feel happy. Your oxytocin level also goes up. Oxytocin is a bonding chemical. It makes you feel calm, it makes you feel contented and it makes you feel good about the person who is touching you. The more you touch someone the more both of your oxytocin levels go up and the more you're likely to stay together.

> **Q:** *How can I get my husband just to give me a cuddle without him always wanting sex to follow?*
>
> **A:** Explain how you feel – that you want cuddling several times a day. Touch is habit-forming, so try to establish the habit and he'll quite probably come to value it for itself.

Rebuilding your sex life

Sex is essentially the most intense form of touching and with the right person it can be hugely beneficial. However, when you're depressed you may not feel very much like sex, and if you're on certain antidepressants you may find they lower your sex drive even further. So it may be a very difficult time for your sex life.

You need to discuss sex with your partner. If you're not used to talking about sex you may find it embarrassing and, of course, you may feel humiliated by your current situation. Both reactions are understandable but quite unnecessary. Try to be as open as possible.

Sex can certainly play a role in your recovery. By flooding your brain with endorphins it can help combat depression and create a sensation of pleasure and well-being, even euphoria and bliss.

However, men who have reached middle age and beyond need to be aware that sex can actually *cause* depression. It can deplete various chemicals including serotonin (the same neurotransmitter that antidepressants increase). This is known as the 'sexual hangover' and it's as real a phenomenon as the hangover that follows too much alcohol.

> *After sex my wife wanted cuddles and I just wanted to get on with something else. I never felt very lovey-dovey. In fact, I'd feel quite down and my wife would get upset. Then I read about the sexual hangover and it was like: 'Wham! That's so me!' I'd never linked sex with feeling depressed before. Now I've got the hang of the new way of making love our life together has been transformed. The loving feelings never go away.*
>
> **John**

(*For help with relationship problems, see the contact information in Part 5.*)

You and your children

Most children grow up expecting their parents to take care of them. They believe their parents to be invincible. So, understandably, it can come as quite a shock to see you suffering from depression.

Your children may feel anxious, betrayed and even resentful. Your natural inclination will be to protect them from knowing about your condition but, in the real world, you can only do so much. They're going to know something is wrong and your best course of action is to explain to them in a way appropriate to their ages.

If your depression makes you withdrawn your children may also worry that you don't love them any more:

- Try to give them plenty of hugs. If you're lying in bed or on the sofa feeling down why not all cuddle together?

- Reassure them about your love at every opportunity.

- Ask your partner and relatives to explain to the children how much you love them.

- Take advantage of 'okay' days to have quality time with your children – but also reserve some for yourself.

Don't feel guilty about being a 'bad' parent. You didn't choose to be depressed any more than you would have chosen to have a broken leg – and you're certainly nothing unusual. Millions of parents suffer from depression. If your children ask you questions, try to answer them as honestly as possible considering their ages. They may ask you the same questions over and over again. That's just the way children show their anxiety.

You may also like to think about ways you can enlist your children's help with tasks you no longer have the energy to tackle. Apart from anything else, the children will feel needed and develop a sense of self-worth rather than feeling left out.

MYTH: Boys shouldn't be cuddled by their parents especially not when they reach the age of about 11.

FACT: Everybody needs physical contact throughout life (see the section on the importance of touch on page 200).

Tips for setting tasks

- Make a list of the most vital tasks and, as far as possible, let your children choose the ones they'd like to do.

- Make sure the chores are appropriate to their ages and abilities.

- If you have two or more children get them to work together on the bigger tasks – for example, one can clear the table and dispose of leftovers while another washes up.

- Forget about things that aren't a priority and don't expect the children to complete tasks as well as you would have done.

- Always thank your children and praise them for their help.

Of course, there's going to come a time – hopefully, quite quickly – when you start to feel more energetic again. Naturally, you're going to want things to return to the way they were before you became ill. But don't expect too much too soon:

- Don't suddenly change the routines that were established when you were depressed – take things gradually.

- Don't immediately overturn any rules your partner may have established when you were ill.

- Don't try to force your way back into your children's schedules. Rather, explain how much you've missed doing things together and ask them what *they* would like.

- Don't suddenly take on too much responsibility for the children all at once – ease your way back into things.

- Above all, as you get better, make sure you still have some time to yourself.

You and your relatives and friends

If they don't have any experience of depression, friends and relatives are likely to be a little wary of you. They're going to be watching for signs that you're 'going crazy' and asking themselves questions such as:

- Shall I go and see her/him or will that be too tiring?

- Should I let on that I know about the depression?

- Should I discuss depression, or will that make things worse?

Also, once you get better they're going to be asking themselves whether it's all right to say or do something in case it might cause a relapse. To a large extent, they're going to take their cue from you. So it's going to be up to you to reassure them and define the way they need to behave. For example, if you're secretive they'll imagine that you do, indeed, have things to hide. It's far better to be frank and open and to explain what treatment you're having and what it involves. You could suggest that they read this book or another from the list in Part 5, Chapter 16.

Don't imagine for one moment that you're boring or that you're a burden to other people. Most people will be sympathetic and even, privately, a little intrigued. At worst, you're not going to be the life and soul of the party, but your presence certainly isn't going to stop anyone else having a good time. When you're asked to join other people don't turn the invitation down on the grounds that you'll 'spoil' things. If people have asked you to go it's because they want you. If you feel up to going, go. Make the effort.

With luck, you'll have one or two particular people you can discuss your problems with in a fairly profound manner. Some people are very happy to take on that role. They're good listeners and they like to help. You'll know instinctively who these people are. It's almost certain that, among your circle of friends and relatives, there will be others who have suffered from depression, or are suffering from it right now. You may be able to get together and create your own support group. For example, you could:

- Agree you can phone one another at any time of the day or night if you're feeling bad.

- Agree you'll draw attention to any strange behaviour in one another – for example, non-stop speaking that signals the start of an 'up' phase in bipolar disorder.

- Agree that you'll all cut down drinking. For example, when you go to the pub together you could all drink halves instead of pints.

- Organize exercise sessions together.

It may be that some of your friends and relatives will blame your partner (if you have one) for your depression. That's an understandable reaction. So put them right, otherwise quite unnecessary tensions are going to be created. Above all, explain how difficult it is for your partner to live with you and ask your relatives and friends to support your partner (or other carer) by taking on some of the tasks you can no longer manage while depressed.

When relationships end

It can happen that relationships break up under the strain of depression. Or it may even be that you became depressed because of the break-up of a relationship. Either way, it's always very sad when a relationship comes to an end, especially if it's been a long relationship.

These are some of the signs that a break-up has damaged your self-esteem:

- You find it difficult to get on with things.

- You find it difficult to take responsibility and prefer others to do that for you.

- You don't take up new opportunities.

- You put yourself down all the time.

- You become emotional and withdrawn.

If this does happen to you here are some things you could try:

- Experiment with a completely new style. For example, you could change your hair or buy those clothes you always wanted but which your partner hated.

- Catch up with those friends and relatives you may not have had much time for in the past.

- Pamper yourself a little bit with presents to yourself and a few treats and luxuries.

- Make a list of all your good points.

- Set yourself some goals that are attainable and yet exciting and stimulating.

- Don't give yourself a hard time.

- Try to look forward to the new things that lie in store for you.

(To get more help following the break-up of a relationship, see Part 5.)

Rebuilding your life alone

If you're living alone and finding life lonely and even pointless it may help to remember that some people are perfectly happy in that situation and wouldn't want it to change. Is there some secret they possess? In fact, they're people who focus on what they see as the positive side to their situation. You, too, should try not to focus too

touch with your family again but don't feel able to initiate things maybe a more distant member of the family or a mutual friend could try to act as a go-between.

If you don't like living alone but don't want to or can't live with your family, give some thought to sharing a flat or house with friends. Alternatively, take a look through the flat-sharing adverts in your local newspaper. You may be able to find somewhere to live and make new friends all at the same time.

In the meantime, while you're waiting for that special person to come along, you may be able to find the human contact and emotional warmth you crave through an activity that brings you into contact with people, such as voluntary work (see Chapter 9, page 237). Apart from anything else, the more you get out and about and the more people you meet, the greater the chance of falling in love. There are specialist organizations out there that can help you, like the Single Concern Group and the National Council for the Divorced and Separated (see Part 5 for details).

You might also like to consider getting a pet you can stroke and cuddle. Of course, they're called pets precisely because they're there to be petted. Some of us are dog people and some of us are cat people and some of us are both. They're the nation's favourite pets and there's no doubt they're the best when it comes to touch. If you're not able to keep a pet you might like to consider doing voluntary work at an animal rescue centre or something like that. Another possibility would be to take up horse riding. The idea of animals helping to treat depression may sound trivial but it has proven benefits.

Self-help groups

Once you feel robust enough to go to new places and meet new people you might like to consider joining a self-help group. These groups are invaluable for anyone suffering from depression but especially:

- If you live alone.

- If you don't have anyone with whom you can discuss your problems and feelings.

You'll be in the company of other men and women who are experiencing the same feelings as you. Some will just be starting their battles with depression, some will be making progress and some will almost be back to normal. In this atmosphere you'll be able to:

• Express your feelings.

• Hear about other people's experiences.

• Gain useful, practical information.

There may be people on antidepressants only. There may be other people on psychotherapy only. Still others may be using both. There may also be some following quite different paths. By listening to what they all have to say you'll be better placed to make decisions about your own treatment. Overall, these groups can be an invaluable resource and a vital source of support and comfort. And you may make some very good friends, too.

Self-help groups are usually headed by a volunteer who has already gone some way to overcoming depression. However, these people are not trained therapists. For that, you'll need to see a professional.

(*For information about self-help groups in your area, see Part 5, Chapter 13.*)

Towards a happier life

You now have a lot of 'tools' at your disposal with which to tackle depression. Don't give up just because they don't give instant results. It all takes time and the longer you've been depressed the longer it takes to get better. Just keep in mind the advice that **the more things you do the more successful you're likely to be**.

In the next chapter we'll be looking at some of the final pieces of the 'jigsaw' including how you can protect yourself from stress and how you can set about solving the problems that may have been responsible for the depression in the first place. Try to keep as positive as you can. Every day that goes by brings you a step closer to the normal life and happiness you deserve.

9

Remaining free from depression

If you've been following all the advice in this book for a while there's an excellent chance that you're no longer feeling so depressed or even depressed at all. Hopefully that is the case. Now you have to make your life as happy as possible and keep it that way. How? That's what we'll be looking at in this chapter.

Protecting yourself from stress

Modern life has many advantages but it's also terribly demanding. We're all more stressed than we realize, which is a very bad thing. Stress increases the level of the hormone cortisol which is associated with feelings of hopelessness, failure, anxiety and depression. It could also be responsible for causing quite a few other health problems in the future as well. So in order to keep depression at bay you need to tackle stress.

Of course, it's not possible to avoid all stress and you're not necessarily stressed every time you're in a stressful situation. It's when you can't cope with all the things life is throwing at you that there's a problem. In other words, you can help to avoid feeling stressed if you do your best to keep away from stressful situations or improve your coping techniques – or both.

Tips for reducing stress

In Chapter 8 we looked at some of the techniques you can use to reduce stress in your job and the same principles apply in all aspects of life:

- Get organized. A diary is just as important for noting a visit to the school play, a dental appointment or a dinner with friends as it is for a business appointment.

- Say goodbye to perfectionism. For example, will your child really enjoy her birthday party more if you get all the lettering on the cake exactly the same size?

- Learn to get help. In the business world the word is 'delegate' but the same principles apply at home. If you can't cope, ask your partner, friends, relatives, neighbours and, if appropriate, your children for assistance. If there's no one you feel you can turn to take a look at the support networks and helplines in Part 5.

How to stop worrying about the unknown

We all worry about the unknown. From time to time you may be asking yourself these sorts of questions:

- Will I be able to make new friends when I move?

- Will it hurt when I have this medical procedure?

Quite often the reality proves to be less frightening than we'd imagined. So if you often worry about the unknown, the solution is to try to turn it into the 'known' instead. Then the situation won't be so stressful. How can you do that? Here are some ideas:

- Always try to talk to people who have experience of the matter.

- Read books on the subject.

- Look for information on the internet; in particular, see if there are any internet chat rooms that are relevant.

- If you're training towards a particular goal aim to tackle something harder – then the goal itself will seem easy.

Improving your coping techniques

There are all kinds of techniques for coping with stress but, in general, they tend to amount to ways of stepping back a bit before reacting. Unfortunately, we all have our very own 'buttons' that, when pressed, cause us to overreact and become more upset, irritable, angry and stressed than we need to. In order to try to stop that happening you need to build up your 'tranquillity balance' by finding time to relax *every day*. It could be, for example:

- Lying on the sofa listening to some relaxing music.

- Lying in a bath or jacuzzi.

- Taking a stroll in the woods.

- Sharing a meal with friends.

- The relaxation exercises given in Part 5, Chapter 12.

- Yoga (see Chapter 6).

- Meditation (see Chapter 6).

Stop 'Type A' behaviour

There is a style of behaviour known as Type A. Type As are: always in a hurry, highly competitive, ambitious, easily irritated – and stressed.

They contrast with Type Bs who are: calm, tranquil, easy-going, patient – and not stressed.

If you're a Type A it will be better for your mental and physical health if you can become a Type B. Is it possible to make such a fundamental change? If you're an extreme Type A you'll probably never manage to act like a Type B when taken by surprise. However, in all other circumstances it should be possible to become far more like a Type B by making a conscious effort.

For example, if you usually become impatient in a queue then see if you can find a way of enjoying the experience and/or using the time usefully. Maybe you could talk to the person next to you, for example, or read a book.

Here are some other ideas:

- Make a point of listening to other people and reflecting on what they have to say before replying.

- Try to find something you agree with rather than something to disagree with.

- Remember that every force creates an equal and opposite force. In other words, if you're aggressive towards someone you can expect them to be aggressive back. Be conciliatory yourself and meet aggression from others with conciliation.

- When someone tells you a problem don't automatically think you have to find a solution – sometimes all they want is a little sympathy.

- Ask other people to mention it when you're acting in Type A style.

- When the telephone rings, or when somebody says something you disagree with – or in fact whenever you face a potentially stressful situation – don't do anything until you've gone into 'protection mode' (see below).

Protection mode

You're probably quite good at protecting your physical body. We're sure you fasten your seat belt, for example, and if you cut yourself you probably clean the wound and apply a sticking plaster. But do you take the same care with your mental health?

As soon as anything threatens your self-esteem or your equilibrium try to go into 'protection mode'. Let's see how this works in practice. Suppose somebody criticizes you. In the past you may have reacted with the following kinds of thoughts: 'This is the end'; 'I'll never be any good'; 'I'm a failure'.

However, from now on your first reaction must be: 'This is a dangerous situation for my mental health – I must take care.' The most important piece of advice is this:

Try not to react.

In other words, don't become upset or angry or defensive or aggressive. Simply keep calm and get yourself 'centred'. Of course, it's very easy to write and very hard to do. The following procedure may help:

- Smile outwardly for the other person.

- Smile inwardly for yourself.

- Close your eyes momentarily and breathe into your abdomen.

- Try to imagine that the 'inner you' has floated up and is now looking down on the scene in a benevolent sort of way. In other words, try to detach yourself before answering.

Don't answer until you've done all of that. It will only take a moment. Of course, if you're face to face with someone you're going to have to give an immediate response. If, on the other hand, you've received the criticism in, say, an email, you can spend much longer composing or centring yourself. So what is this feeling of being 'centred'? Basically,

- You feel calm.

- You feel in control of your body and your thoughts.

- You have the belief that you can deal with the situation without having to exert yourself.

- No energy is wasted; everything is to the point.

If you have time before you have to respond, think how you will calmly deal with the situation and visualize the possible ways in which your strategy might go wrong and what your next step will then have to be.

Once you've talked yourself or thought yourself into a more positive frame of mind don't dwell on what happened. It may help to write down what was said to you then screw the paper into a ball and symbolically throw it into the waste paper bin. Episode over!

Dealing with anger

Anger is probably part of the mechanism that has evolved over millions of years to make us capable of an unusual effort. When we're angry we're willing to tackle people and problems we might otherwise be afraid of. So anger can be useful.

But let's look at anger another way. Yes, there are occasions when you may channel anger to some positive end, but in our modern society we're seldom called upon to use superhuman force and we no longer settle disputes physically. We have the law to take care of that. Moreover, acting without thinking may be useful when grappling with a bear but it's entirely inappropriate when you have a disagreement with your partner, for example.

In other words, getting angry is only going to make the situation worse. So try to remain calm and centre yourself. Later, once the crisis has passed, write down any negative thoughts you had and compare them with the different types described in Chapter 6.

Me and my friends were always arguing. I'd come home feeling really down. Now if they say something I don't agree with I just sort of stand back a bit and smile. Then they go: 'Yeah, yeah, you're right,' because they know they're saying something stupid.

Kate

Dealing with panic attacks

When you're suffering from depression you may also have panic attacks. They can be extremely frightening. You may feel:

- Anxious.

- Afraid.

- Breathless.

- Dizzy.

- Sweaty.

- Trembly.

- Heart palpitations.

You may even mistake the symptoms for a heart attack. Don't worry about that. Panic attacks are quite common for all sorts of reasons. Most people experience them at some time.

   If you have these kinds of symptoms the first thing to do is consult your doctor. It may have been a panic attack. It may have been something else. Your doctor is the best person to decide what to do.

If panic attacks are confirmed there are several things you can try to bring them under control and then stop them.

Why do panic attacks happen?

Panic attacks occur when:

- Your subconscious mind thinks it has detected danger.

- Your conscious mind isn't involved.

That's why panic attacks seem to come out of nowhere.

What happens in panic attacks is that the subconscious perceives danger when there is no danger. It makes a mistake. It primes you for urgent action and floods your body with chemicals that aren't appropriate. These account for all the symptoms.

How can these mistakes happen? Early humans had to be ready for predators that suddenly burst out of the bushes. *Thinking* about running was too

---

slow, the subconscious set them running even *before* they knew why.

When you're already very stressed for some reason you're just like those early humans moving warily across the savannah. It doesn't take very much to tip you over into panic. So if someone close to you has died, for example, you may be vulnerable not only to depression but to panic attacks as well.

Once your subconscious has caused a panic attack in a certain situation you may then have more panic attacks in similar situations. If you can identify where or in what circumstances you experience panic attacks you may be able to 'decondition' yourself by making a very conscious effort to relax. In effect you're saying to your subconscious: Look, you made a mistake; see how relaxed I am.

(*To find out more about dealing with panic attacks, see Part 5, Chapter 12.*)

Religion, spirituality and depression

There's no doubt that many people find considerable comfort in their religious and spiritual beliefs when faced with problems, including depression. Indeed, there's evidence that people who regularly attend a place of worship tend to suffer from less depression in the first place.

Of course, you can't just decide to believe in God or a particular religion on the grounds that you might be less likely to get depressed. However, if you do believe in a certain religion but are not active then you might like to consider becoming more involved. Being an active follower of a particular religion can have several advantages:

- Regular contact with other members of the religion.

- Social support and a sense of community (especially helpful if you're living alone).

- A sense of purpose.

- Advice and help from religious leaders.

- Rituals that help carry you through difficult times.

> *MYTH: Only religious people are spiritual.*
>
> **FACT:** It isn't necessary to believe in God to be a spiritual person.

If you are not a member of any religion you can still be a very spiritual person, of course. Religions are organized spiritual beliefs but you may have your own beliefs that are different.

I stopped going to church years ago. Then, on a whim, when I was feeling depressed, I went to a service and everyone was so nice. They even said a prayer for me the following week. They really cared and that made me feel so much better.

Sarah

Q: What can I do to cultivate my spiritual feelings?

A: You might like to read books on the subject and think about what they have to say (see Part 5, Chapter 16). It may also benefit you to get out more often and to get closer to nature and to help others.

Helping others

If you're depressed you've possibly lost your self-esteem, your optimism and your faith in the world. Well, there's no better way of boosting all three than by doing some sort of voluntary work – helping other people, helping animals or helping the environment.

Quite apart from anything else, voluntary work will bring you into contact with other wonderful people who will do much to restore your faith in the human race and in the future. It's all too easy to fall into the trap of despondency when you stand aside and do nothing. You only see the things that are going wrong. So think about getting involved and that way, you'll see all the things that are going right and be a part of those achievements. Everybody has some sort of contribution they can make. You'll feel proud of yourself and so you should.

Practical problem solving

Most experts advise that you shouldn't make any big changes in your life when you're suffering from depression. It's easy to see why they say that. If your judgement is affected you might end up doing something you'll regret later on. However, on the other hand, if your depression is due to the circumstances you're in it's very hard to see how you can get better *unless* you make some changes. It's all very well to say that happiness comes from within but it's asking a lot to be happy in an awful situation.

Of course, not every situation can be changed but there are many that can. For example:

- Having to work at a job you hate.

- Neighbours who abuse you.

- A neighbourhood that's dangerous.

- Living with a violent partner.

- Bullying.

Or it could be more general things such as you're not allowed to be yourself or you're not able to live the life you want.

Some people say you can't run away from yourself, but it isn't a question of that. It's a question of getting away from an intolerable situation. Yes, if you become expert at the techniques of self-therapy you may be able to endure these kinds of things and more without becoming depressed, but it's going to be a whole lot easier if you can solve the problem that led to your depression and, if necessary, get out of the situation altogether.

In order to solve a problem you first need to identify it very specifically. Then:

- Set a clear goal.

- Set out the steps by which you can progress from your current position to your goal.

- If you can't see the steps very clearly try working *backwards* from your goal.

- Don't neglect *lateral* thinking. That's to say, not necessarily trying to move directly towards your goal but coming at it in a more roundabout, creative manner.

- Research solutions by asking experts and by consulting books and the internet; you can also try 'brainstorming' for solutions with friends.

- If you can't see a solution try to stop thinking about it for a time and let your subconscious work on the problem; a solution may then suddenly come into your mind.

- Be willing to try several approaches simultaneously.

Use your insight

Once you've had depression and learned all about it you're quite likely to start spotting depression in other people. That would hardly be surprising because depression is a large and growing problem. If you see people who are depressed don't hold back from sharing your experiences with them. It will make them feel a lot better to know you understand what they're going through.

Remember:

- Most problems have a solution.

- If you can't find the solution on your own – get help.

- If you can't cope with a situation never be ashamed to admit it.

- If you need to get away from a situation then do so in a responsible manner if you possibly can.

> *I was living with a man who used to beat me up. I tried lots of things including counselling but nothing did any good. It went on like that for two years until I left him. I was one of the lucky ones because he didn't bother me any more. I'm happy now but I never could have been if I'd have stayed.*
>
> **Jackie**

Continuing the good work

Although you'll probably stop taking antidepressants at some point, there are certain other things you should never stop. They're not just treatments for depression they're also part of a healthy depression-resistant lifestyle. Be sure to continue to:

• Eat a healthy diet.

• Avoid stress where possible.

• Get plenty of fresh air and sunlight.

• Follow an exercise programme.

• Practise self-therapy/positive thinking.

• Make time for relationships.

• Drink alcohol only in moderation.

• Tackle problems when you can.

It's important to continue with as many different approaches as possible in order to minimize the possibility of a relapse. If you depend on antidepressants alone, for example, you're much more likely to have depression again than if you combine antidepressants with psychotherapy. And the risk will be reduced still further if you continue with self-help.

REMEMBER

There's an excellent chance you'll never get depressed again if you adopt a lifestyle that incorporates all the things you've learned in this book.

What happens if I have a relapse?

If your depression does ever come back there's no need for despondency. It isn't because of some 'defect' in you. The important thing is to tackle depression in as many different ways as possible.

However, before you jump to the conclusion that you're getting depressed again, are you sure you're not experiencing withdrawal symptoms associated with antidepressants? If you've only just come off antidepressants that could easily be the case (see Chapter 8). Discuss the possibility with your doctor.

If you finished with antidepressants but didn't have psychotherapy because of the long National Health Service (NHS) waiting list ask your doctor to push for you to be given treatment as soon as possible. If you have the financial resources you may want to think about private treatment (see Part 2, Chapter 4). Also enquire about the possibility of psychotherapy by CD or computer.

In the meantime, take another look at the self-therapy section in Part 2, Chapter 6 and keep working on the techniques. Don't neglect all the other self-help techniques in this book, either. When you use everything together you attack depression in a tremendously powerful way.

In the next section we'll be looking at the inspiring stories of people who have beaten depression.

Part 4: From the Postbag

10

Your stories

It was my friend at the young mum's club who made me go to the doctor. She recognized the signs because she'd had depression after her first baby. She even came to the surgery with me to make sure I went. I would have gone anyway because I was fed up of feeling rotten. The doctor was really nice but she told me there was no magic wand. I saw a counsellor and I had tablets. The health visitor helped as well because at times I really felt like a failure as a mother. I'm fine now. I mean, I have off days like everyone else but I know what they are and I just think things will feel different tomorrow. They always do but if I ever felt the depression was coming back I'd do something about it straight away. I'm not brave so why suffer when you don't have to?

Tracy

At times I feel all right and then it just strikes me. I can be at the school gates talking to the other mums and having a laugh and then, walking home with the pushchair, I just want to have a good cry. I come home and just sit, even though there's a hundred things that need doing. I can sit for hours feeling numb, as though there's no point and then all the things I've done wrong, little things that half of me knows don't matter, just go round and round in my head and I squirm. I can be like that right up to the time when my daughter needs collecting and all I've done all day is see to the baby. It's as though all the energy has drained out of me.

Lisa

Looking back I'm ashamed of the times I've criticized other people for it. In a way it happening to me was a fair punishment. You think depression is what happens to other people, stupid people. You don't realize your mistake till it happens to you. And I've got everything to be happy about, more than I ever expected, so it just shows you. I know that was what my partner thought, that I had a lot to be thankful for. He kept booking things to cheer me up but I couldn't be bothered. That's not the way it works, that you just need cheering up. I just started to feel there was no point to anything. Even tea seemed to lose it's taste and I love a cup of tea. They say it affects people in different ways. For me everything just became pointless. I got private treatment and they were very good and I feel more like my old self now but I've learned a lesson. The hard way!

Janice

*The worst part was feeling I couldn't cope
at work. I tried not to let it show at home
but I knew my wife knew something was
wrong. Afterwards, when it all came out,
she told me she thought I was having an
affair because I was so silent and different
from my usual self. At first, when my boss
asked me what was wrong, I felt as though
I was being persecuted but he persevered.
Eventually he told me he valued me and
that was why he wanted me to get some
help. I felt terrible, as though I'd been
found out in something shameful, but I did
as he said. The relief when the psychiatrist
explained what was happening was
indescribable. It took six months to get back
to normal but after the first month I could
see light at the end of the tunnel. Now
I would tell anyone, don't wait. There's no
virtue in suffering and the help is there if
you reach for it. In my case it was old
wounds to blame but I know of at least two
other people who've just become depressed
out of the blue. Whatever the reason,
treatment works. I really regret what I put
myself and others through because I was
ashamed to admit how I felt.*

Dave

11

Your letters

All letters sent to *This Morning* are confidential. The following letters have been created from the hundreds I receive each week.

Dear Denise,

I just don't know where to turn. I've been married for 20 years and have two lovely daughters, but have been unhappy for the best part of the last 18–20 years. I couldn't leave with two children and nowhere to go but he won't go either. He lives a single man's life and goes out all the time. Sometimes he doesn't come back for days. I had an unhappy childhood, too, as I was abused by an uncle but when I told my parents they didn't do anything about it.

Most of the time I wish I had never been born. I dream of winning the lottery so I can take my girls away and try to start afresh. Sorry for moaning on but I want to run away and be someone else. I haven't talked to anyone – I have no one.

Dear X

I was so sorry to read about the problems you've been having. You sound so disappointed and angry with life and my heart goes out to you. Given that you say you've been unhappy for something approaching 20 years there must have been so many experiences that you've been prevented from enjoying, and to feel this blanket of depression over everything you do must be a terrible burden. Because you have felt dissatisfied for so long you can't remember what it is like to feel any differently and can't imagine finding the courage to change your life but I promise you it can be done. Now I think you need some outside help. What you need is the opportunity to explore your own feelings and to be supported. A counsellor can't solve your problems for you or tell you what to do, but he or she can help you to understand your feelings a little more so that you find ways of coping better with the stresses and strains of life.

Your GP may be able to refer you for counselling. If not I suggest that you talk to Marriage Care (0845 660 6000). They really can help you sort out your feelings towards your marriage. If you decide that it is really over, the Citizens Advice Bureau (**www.citizensadvice. org.uk**) will advise you on your legal and housing rights and help you work out how you can exist financially when you separate. In the meantime Careline (0845 122 8622) and SANELINE (0845 767 8000) both offer support and advice to anyone suffering from depression. They are on hand to listen and offer suggestions to how you might cope with the feelings you have.

I know that right now it may feel as if you will never get better, never lose the fear and isolation you feel, never again know what it is to be truly happy, but I promise you as someone who has known depression that there is hope and that you do have every chance of learning how to live rather than simply exist.

Dear Denise,

I am 15 years old. I have felt really depressed for a few years now. I told my doctor but he didn't take me seriously. All he did was send me to a psychiatrist which didn't help. Recently my mum caught me sobbing and I confided in her which resulted in her taking me to a psychotherapist. I left after a few sessions as it was not helping either. My parents think I am fine now but this is only because I put on a front.

I haven't liked or loved myself in a long time. In fact for a long time I have hated myself – my face, my personality, my everything. I feel there is this cloud hanging over me all the time. I'm sick of it. Please help.

Dear X

Thank you for your email. I was so sorry to read about the problems you've been having. You sound very unhappy and alone and my heart goes out to you.

Clearly you've been battling with depression for a few years and I imagine you must feel very scared that things aren't improving. I know what it is to feel overwhelmed by one's feelings and to feel frightened too that it will never pass.

However, I know from experience that eventually we learn how to understand and deal with these feelings. At the moment you are on the threshold of life and that can be scary. You have become a woman and that means there have been hormonal and other changes to deal with. It's a lot to cope with at once so no wonder you sometimes feel confused.

The good news is that depression is treatable. You say that your GP didn't take your feelings seriously, but I think that he/she must have done because they referred you to a psychiatrist. You say you've also seen a psychotherapist and that didn't help either so I'm wondering if the trouble, in each case, was that you couldn't share your feelings because you felt somehow guilty to feel as you do. Remember that most people have a time in their lives when they feel as you do now. You're not alone and there's no need to feel guilty about something which is not your fault. Therapy does take time, and I wouldn't have expected you to notice any significant change in your mood after a couple of sessions. It takes time to trust in your counsellor, especially when you are confiding such difficult feelings. I would really urge you to try again and give it a really good go this time.

You are obviously a sensitive and intelligent young woman and I am sure that if you stick with it you will start to make headway so that you can move on in your life. You have so much to look forward to once you get this difficult time behind you.

I am not sure whereabouts in the country you live so if you contact Youth Access (020 8772 9900) they will tell you about counselling services in your area which cater especially for young people. In the meantime I would suggest that you contact Careline (0845 122 8622) who offer confidential telephone support to any young person. Finally I would urge you to talk to your parents again and let them know how you really feel. As a parent myself I can safely say that I would much prefer to know that a child of mine was unhappy. Your parents clearly love you very much and I am sure they would want to be there for you.

I know that it may be impossible for you to contemplate a brighter future at the moment but I promise you that it is out there, waiting for you to put your trust in someone who can help you get through this. I have absolute faith in your ability to come through and I am rooting for you all the way.

Dear Denise,

I am 33, single and live on my own. I have a few friends but they have either all settled down or have lots of other friends and they don't need me. I've only ever had one proper boyfriend and that was years ago. I would love to have someone to love me and have children but I know that that will never happen.

I have been off work for weeks now and the only person I speak to is my mum. I keep trying but I keep getting rejected at work and passed over for promotions. Other people who have been there for a lot less time than me get the jobs. I am completely lonely in my personal life. There must be something really wrong with me that no one seems to like me.

A really bad part of me is that I find it really hard to be happy for my friends when they have good news or are telling me about their boyfriends, holidays or promotions. I have put on a lot of weight recently but have no motivation to lose it. Eating is the only thing I have to do. I feel I have nothing to look forward to. Every now and then I try to do something to make things better but I get another knock back and am more miserable than before. I'm not living but just existing. Any advice would be much appreciated.

Dear X

To feel that you are 'existing' and not living and
are unable to move forward, despite your best
efforts must be deeply frustrating and my heart
goes out to you.

You can't deal with everything all at once
but what is essential is that you are supported
right now so that you can begin to tackle each
problem step by step. I think that your first
move should be to talk your feelings through
with someone. At the moment I can imagine that
you might feel overwhelmed and confused by
the enormity of your situation and puzzled as to
how you can sort it all out. I think it would help
to reassure you and allow you to work out
where to begin if you confided in an
understanding and experienced third party. A
counsellor would help you explore ways to make
positive changes to your life. It might be worth
starting with your GP because it's possible you
may be suffering with depression. Your GP
could also refer you to a counsellor who could
really help you make progress. If counselling
through your GP isn't an option then there are
helplines available. If you can afford private
counselling I would suggest that you contact

the British Association for Counselling and
Psychotherapy (01788 550899) and/or
Counselling and Psychotherapy in Scotland
(COSCA) (**www.cosca.org.uk**) for details of
therapists in your area.

My second suggestion is to make a list of the
things you want to achieve. Where do you want
to be in say, three years' time? What would your
life look and be like? What would you be doing?
Where would you be? What would you need to
do in order to reach those goals? That should
give you a starting point but begin by setting
smaller goals, for instance, eating more healthily,
and tick these off one by one. I did this at a very
unhappy time in my life and although I only
managed to achieve about 3 out of 10 having the
list helped a lot.

One of the areas that seems to be causing
you particular concern is your job. You say that
you keep getting passed over for promotion,
with newer staff members being given the jobs
instead. Do you know why this is? I would
certainly urge you to bring this up with your
manager so you can ask some questions. Try to
make it as positive as you can – simply say that
you haven't been selected for promotion and
could they offer some constructive criticism as

you would like to improve your chances in future. Stand back from your job and ask yourself if it's where you really want to be. What are the things you really like and dislike in your job? What are the things you particularly do well, where do your skills lie? If you could tailor your own job – what would it be, and can your present company offer you the opportunity to get somewhere close to that? Let loose with your imagination and see where it takes you. If you think you might do better elsewhere talk to Learn Direct, an organization with a remit from government to provide high quality post-16 learning, about retraining.

I sense that you have come to expect bad things to happen to you and have lost faith that anything hopeful might arrive. Believe me, it can and it will if you reach out for help.

Dear Denise,

My son was badly bullied throughout his school years. He will be 21 this year and still suffers the mental scars of his school days. He has very low, if any, self-esteem. He has a problem with alcohol, doesn't eat properly and he self-harms.

He constantly has to have a girlfriend but because of how he is they invariably finish with him. He is then gutted, drinks and self-harms. Each girl tells him that he needs to sort himself out but he doesn't, he just goes on to another relationship.

He did see a doctor after a girlfriend and I persuaded him to go. He was given an appointment with a counsellor but is still waiting. He lies constantly and when the counsellor does get in touch I don't know whether he will really go.

I am at the end of my tether and don't know which way to turn. I have tried to talk to him and get him to get help with his problem but he seems set on this self-destruct course. He has told me he wants to be dead and I fear this will happen one day.

Dear X

I was so sorry to read about the worries you
have for your son. As parents we want to see our
children happy, safe and secure in their lives and
I appreciate just how distressing it can be if they
seem lost or troubled. The teenage years can be a
very confusing time in a young person's life,
regardless of anything else that may be
happening. School, hormones, peer pressure and
relationships can be enough to plunge some
young people into the depths of depression and
in your son's case it sounds as if he is still
dealing with the legacy of the bullying he
experienced at school.

As we grow older we gain the experience
and strength to deal with things better – young
people often find it much harder to articulate
their feelings or make sense of them. It can be a
terribly painful time and its little wonder that
your son is struggling so much with his feelings.
One of the characteristics of a depressed person
is that they withdraw into themselves and away
from those around them, which often leaves
friends and family feeling excluded, hurt and
powerless to help. Don't take this to heart. The
impression I get is that your son cares for you

very much, and if he pushes you away when you try to help then this is probably more to with a sense of guilt about behaving in the way that he is and not because he doesn't appreciate your concern. Although your support of him may not appear to be having much impact on his outlook, you being there will be vital to his recovery. Speaking of his depression, Spike Milligan said that while in the midst of his illness he would ignore and fight against those who cared for him but that ultimately it was their love that kept him going, even if he didn't realize it at the time. It may seem as if nothing is shifting but don't underestimate the power of your love and support.

If your son is defensive when you try to talk to him it may be that he isn't ready or able to address his difficulties right now. Often, one has to get to rock bottom before one can start coming back up, so don't be surprised or shocked if your son's situation continues for a while before he begins taking control. If he can accept that he needs help and attends counselling then there is no reason why he won't be able to turn his life around. So don't lose heart. If he would talk to a helpline then Get Connected is there especially for people of his age. They will understand how he feels and give him support. I would recommend that you talk to someone who will discuss with you the best way to deal with the problems your son is having, and offer you the opportunity to share how all of this is affecting you. Parentline can offer guidance and support to parents under stress, and can be contacted on 0808 800 2222 on weekdays during normal office hours. I would also recommend The Family Contact Line who are open from 10 a.m. to 10 p.m. every weekday on 0161 941 4011.

I hope this helps a little. In the meantime you are in my thoughts and I wish you all the very best.

You are absolutely right – I have been where you are and I do empathize entirely with the way you're feeling. I remember a period during the depths of depression where I would run my hands under scalding hot water with the crazy idea that for a few seconds, the pain of the scald would set me free of the terrible pain I felt inside. The depression I felt was something I doubted I would ever be free of. I also felt worthless, that I was a burden to others and that I would never amount to anything or be happy. But I now know this was the illness making me feel this way, not reality. I have had such wonderful happiness since then and I know that you can too if you can just find that little bit of belief.

You may disagree with me, but I believe that there was a reason that you were found and that you survived your overdose. Whether that is the case or not, you are alive and have been given a second chance at life, and it is entirely within your grasp to make it a happier, healthier and more fulfilling one than before. All you need do is accept the help on offer. There are a number of counselling services in and around where you live and Careline (0845 122 8622) will help you find the nearest one. I would also urge you to consider joining a self-help/support group so that you can interact with other people who suffer from depression. Don't assume that a depression support group would be depressing – they can actually be immensely supportive and invaluable. Above all, trust your doctor. If he or she gives you reason to doubt them have the courage to change to another. A good doctor is essential to navigate a way through depression. And there is a way, I promise you. At the moment you feel you are a surrounded by a wall. But there is a door in that wall, and when you find it a new life is waiting on the other side.

Part 5:
More Help
at Hand

We hope this book has been able to help you. But it's just the beginning. There's a great deal of additional support available to you. Don't ignore it. If you need to speak to someone there are telephone helplines for depression and all the other issues that can be associated with depression. You'll be speaking to sympathetic and well-trained women and men who will listen very carefully to you and do their best to advise and inform you. You can even chat with other sufferers on the internet, which can be a tremendous relief. If you want to learn more about depression there are books and websites that can tell you all you need to know. And if you want to do the maximum to help yourself then all the necessary resources are provided here.

To find out more about overcoming anxiety or a panic attack, see Chapter 12.

To get in touch with other people who are suffering or to get support to help look after someone who is depressed, see Chapter 13.

To speak to someone right now who can help, see Chapter 14.

To find out about internet resources, see Chapter 15.

For a list of useful books to find out more information, see Chapter 16.

12

Quick reference guide to emergency relaxation

When you're suddenly overcome by feelings of anxiety or panic for no obvious reason it can be very frightening, and lonely. All around you see other people carrying on as normal while you're gripped by what seems to be a presentiment of tragedy and doom. In this chapter we look at some of the 'emergency' techniques that should help you to get through and bring the episodes to as quick an end as possible.

However, sometimes, of course, these feelings do stem from a very real problem. So it's also important for you to tackle that situation if you possibly can. If it's a problem that can be solved but not by you on your own, don't be ashamed to seek help. Later in this section you'll find contact details for all kinds of resources. If you have family and friends don't be afraid to ask them for help, either. Most people would want to help and would almost certainly feel upset at being left out by you.

Breathing exercises

If you can get control of your breathing then the rest of your body and your mind will follow.

The invisible balloon

The first exercise comes from Japan, a country renowned for its martial arts specialists and others who can perform seemingly superhuman feats. In fact, there's nothing superhuman about this exercise but it is highly effective.

Step 1 Sit upright without resting against the back of your chair. Bring your hands up about 6 inches apart and 6 inches in front of your mouth and curve them as if holding an invisible balloon. As you breathe out through your mouth imagine that the balloon is getting bigger and as you breathe in through your mouth imagine that it gets smaller. As you breathe, so your hands move in and out. Gradually let your hands come closer and closer together as if you are gently squashing the balloon. Finally let them touch.

Step 2 Now, with your hands in an attitude of prayer and your eyes closed breathe through your nose. As you breathe in, imagine that *ki* (energy) is being sucked into your fingertips and as you breathe out imagine it is spurting out of your fingertips like water from a fountain. Continue like this for at least three minutes. You should now feel relaxed and energized.

Belly breathing

When you're relaxed your stomach should move in and out as you breathe. However, if you're tense or agitated it may be that your shoulders are moving up and down, something that should only happen when exercising. Here is a way of deliberately restoring 'belly breathing' and, by doing so, helping to overcome feelings of panic:

Place a hand flat over your navel and breathe in through your nose for a count of four in such a way that you can feel your tummy expand and push against your hand (belly breathing). Now breathe out through your nose for a count of seven, while feeling your tummy go back in. Hold for two seconds.

Repeat the cycle for a couple of minutes or until you feel calm again. The essential things is that you take longer breathing out than in. Remember: Out is longest, in is quickest.

Practise the technique several times every day. You'll find it helps you feel more relaxed and reduces the likelihood of a panic attack.

The carbon dioxide method

When you feel anxious or overcome by panic you're likely to hyperventilate. In other words, you breathe too rapidly which, paradoxically, can actually make you feel short of breath. Hyperventilation can also result in:

- Dizziness.

- Heart palpitations.

- Chest pains.

- Weakness.

To restore the correct balance of oxygen and carbon dioxide try the following suggestions:

- Keep a paper bag with you. When a panic attack comes on, hold the bag over your face and breathe in and out so that you re-inhale the carbon dioxide that you're exhaling.

- Try to hold your breath for 10 to 15 seconds. Repeat 6 times.

The exercise method

Quite a lot of people instinctively pace up and down when they're stressed or agitated and this is a good thing. If you're having a panic attack shift your weight from foot to foot as rhythmically as possible (you can jog if you like) while breathing in and out through your nose.

Skin contact

Skin contact, as we've seen, is very reassuring. If you're with someone you know well enough, take hold of their hand. If you're on your own or among strangers you can still derive some reassurance from touching your own skin. If it sounds a little daft to you then you might like to know that the tough guys and girls who go diving under the sea hold their own wrists as a way of inducing calm, relaxing their breathing and conserving air. Here are four suggestions:

- Take hold of somebody's hand.

- Take hold of your own hand (palm of one hand against the back of the other).

- Circle your left wrist between the fingers and thumb of your right hand, and your right wrist between the fingers and thumb of your left hand.

- Hold your hands a little in front of you, fingers slightly spread, and press the tips of the fingers of one hand lightly against their opposite numbers.

Physical relaxation

This way of inducing physical relaxation goes back thousands of years but has never been improved on.

Step 1 Lie face up on your bed or the floor with your feet a little more than shoulder width apart, feet turned comfortably out, arms a little way from your sides, palms up. For comfort, you can put a small cushion under your neck and, if you have back problems, under each knee. Close your eyes for a few minutes and belly breathe as described above.

Step 2 In this phase you first tense and then relax 15 parts of your body in sequence:

1 Feet – Curl your toes away from you. Hold for a few seconds, then release.

2 Calves – Curl your toes towards you. Hold for a few seconds, then release.

3 Knees – Push the backs of your knees against the bed/floor. Hold for a few seconds, then release.

4 Thighs – Rotate your feet inwards so your toes face each other. Hold for a few seconds, then release.

5 Abdomen – Breathe out while pulling your navel in and squeezing your buttocks together. Hold for a few seconds, then release.

6 Solar plexus – Breathe out while pulling your navel back towards your spine. Hold for a few seconds, then release.

7 Chest – Breathe in, expanding your rib cage to its maximum. Hold for a few seconds, then release.

8 Spine – Push your spine against the bed/floor. Hold for a few seconds, then release.

9 Hands – Make fists. Hold for a few seconds, then release.

10 Forearms – Press your wrists against the bed/floor. Hold for a few seconds, then release.

11 Upper arms – Press your elbows against the bed/floor. Hold for a few seconds, then release.

12 Neck – Press your chin against the top of your breastbone. Hold for a few seconds, then release.

13 Head – Press the back of your head against the bed/floor. Hold for a few seconds, then release.

14 Jaw – With your lips together, press your tongue against the roof of your mouth. Hold for a few seconds, then release.

15 Eyes – Squeeze your upper and lower lids together. Hold for a few seconds, then release.

Each sequence of contracting and releasing can last anything from around ten seconds up to around thirty seconds so that all of Step 2 should take between three and ten minutes. At the end you should feel very relaxed and sleepy. If not, you can do Step 2 all over again.

13

Support networks

When you're depressed, or living with someone who's depressed, one of the most important things you can do is talk things over with other people who understand and who can also help with knowledgeable practical advice and support. Unfortunately, only a very lucky few have that possibility. That's where support networks come in. The whole idea of support networks is that you can:

- Meet other sufferers face to face, share experiences and compare treatments.

- Meet other carers face to face, discuss your problems and, perhaps, arrange rotas and the like for helping one another.

- Meet online via chat rooms and message boards.

Useful support networks

Depression Alliance
212 Spitfire Studios
63–71 Collier Street
London N1 9BE
Tel: 0845 123 2320 (this is not a helpline)
email: information@depressionalliance.org
website: **www.depressionalliance.org**
The Depression Alliance has around 60 self-help support groups in Britain. Some are very small, while others are larger and in addition to meeting for mutual support may have invited speakers. Some meet weekly and others monthly.

Meetings begin with members talking about themselves for a few minutes. By listening you'll get to know the circumstances of the other members and perhaps learn some useful things. You'll also be invited to talk about yourself for five minutes or so. You may feel rather awkward about this idea the first week but you'll probably find it easier as time goes on. You're certainly not compelled to say anything if you don't want to.

Discussions are led by group organizers. They are not trained therapists but people who have volunteered to help set up and run the group. They'll be people who are suffering from depression themselves but they're likely to be quite knowledgeable.

If there isn't a group close to you, you can nevertheless still register and, once sufficient people in your area have shown interest, a new self-help support group may be established. In the meantime there is also a pen-friend scheme.

The Association for Post Natal illness
145 Dawes Road
Fulham
London SW6 7EB
Tel: 020 7386 0868
email: info@apni.org
website: **www.apni.org**
This organization has a network of volunteers througout the country.

The Bipolar Fellowship Scotland
Studio 1061
Mile End Mill
Abbeymill Business Centre
Seedhill Road
Paisley PA1 1TJ
Tel: 0141 560 2050
website: **www.bipolarscotland.org.uk**
This organization has various support groups.

Cruse Bereavement Care

PO Box 800
Richmond
Surrey TW9 1RG
Tel: 0845 477 9400
email: helpline@cruse.org.uk
website: **www.crusebereavementcare.org.uk**
Cruse has branches througout the UK for those grieving the loss of a loved one.

Gingerbread One Parent Families

255 Kentish Town Road
London NW5 2LX
Tel: 0800 018 5026
email: info@oneparentfamilies.org.uk
website: **www.gingerbread.org.uk**
Gingerbread and One Parent Families have merged to create a new, larger self-help organization for single parents who are finding their situation a strain and would like to meet up with other single parents in their area for mutual support.

A country-wide mutual support group for depression sufferers can be found at: **www.depressionanon.co.uk**
If you're lonely and would like someone to go on holiday with look up: **www.work4travel.co.uk**

You'll normally be asked to register by giving your email address and a nickname. Only after you've done that will you be allowed to join the chat or respond to messages on the notice board. Here are the details of some chat rooms and notice boards dealing with depression:

http://blogs.healthcentral.com/depression
www.deardenise.com
http://depression.about.com/mpboards.htm
www.depressionchat.com
www.depressionforums.org
http://forums.walkers.org
www.ourpeacefulhaven.com
www.sane.org.uk
http://spiritofwisdom.iipbhost.com
www.touchingminds.org

14

Helplines

Support and advice is only a telephone call away. Let's begin with some general helplines for depression.

Breathing Space
Tel: 0800 83 85 87 (6 p.m. to 2 a.m. daily)
Helpline specifically for men in Scotland aged 12 to 40.

Careline
Tel: 0845 122 8622 (10 a.m. to 1 p.m. and 7 p.m. to 10 p.m. Monday to Friday)
National telephone counselling service to relieve mental suffering.

Community Advice and Listening Line
Tel: 0800 132 737 (10 a.m. to 2 p.m. and 7 p.m. to 11 p.m. weekdays; noon to midnight weekends)
Specifically for those with mental health problems in Wales.

Family Contact Line
Tel: 0845 120 3799 (normal hours)

Samaritans

Tel: 08457 90 90 90 (24 hours)

Help for those who feel anxious, depressed and suicidal.

SANELINE

Tel: 0845 767 8000 (1 p.m. to 11 p.m. every day)

SANE is a leading charity for all those affected by depression and other kinds of mental illness. The charity's helpline is called SANELINE and was established in 1992. If you're suffering from depression or living with someone with depression you can get practical information, crisis care and emotional support on the telephone.

Calls are answered by volunteers who have been through a training programme recognized by the Royal College of Psychiatrists. For those who don't speak English very well there's a translation service capable of dealing with over 100 languages. If you have a hearing impairment it's also possible to contact SANELINE using Type Talk via textphone.

The Stress, Anxiety, Depression Confidential Helpline

Tel: 01622 717656 (Noon to 3 p.m. weekdays)
This is a voluntary, self-help organization run by qualified health professionals who also suffer with anxiety and depression. You are guaranteed a sympathetic and knowledgeable ear.

SupportLine

Tel: 020 8554 9004 (hours vary)
SupportLine listens, supports and responds to callers in need of emotional support due to depression or any other reason.

Young Minds

Tel: 0800 018 2138 (10 a.m. to 1 p.m. Mon and Fri; 1 p.m. to 4 p.m. Tues to Thurs)
Helpline for adults concerned about the mental health of a child or young person.

Depression caused by bereavement

Cruse Bereavement Care

Tel: 0845 758 5565 (3 p.m. to 9 p.m. Mon to Fri)
Counselling for those who have lost a loved one.

Depression linked with drugs and alcohol

Al-Anon Family Groups UK and Eire
Tel: 020 7403 0888 (24 hours)
Helpline for the families and friends of problem drinkers.

Drinkline
Tel: 0800 917 8282 (9 a.m. to 11 p.m. weekdays; 6 p.m. to 11 p.m. weekends)
Information and advice for anyone with alcohol problems.

National Drugs Helpline
Tel: 0800 776 600 (24 hours)
Advice and support for anyone misusing drugs and also for their friends and family.

Depression caused by loneliness

Campaign Against Living Miserably
Tel: 0800 585 858 (5 p.m. to 3 a.m. every day)
Telephone counselling for men who are isolated, depressed or suicidal.

Single Concern Group
Tel: 01643 708 008
Advice and support on loneliness and related problems.

Depression caused by relationship problems

Marriage Care
Tel: 0845 660 6000 (10 a.m. to 4 p.m. Mon to Fri)
Advice and support for marriages with problems, based on Catholic teaching.

Parentline
Tel: 0808 800 2222 (24 hours)
Helpline for anyone in a parenting role.

Relate
Tel: 0845 130 4010 (9.30 a.m. to 4.30 p.m. weekdays)
Counselling for couples and families.

Depression caused by sexual abuse

Family Matters
Tel: 01474 537392 (9 a.m. to 5 p.m. weekdays, otherwise answerphone)
Counsellors are specially trained to help all those who were sexually abused as children.

Rape Crisis Federation
Tel: 0115 900 3560 (10 a.m. to 4 p.m. weekdays)
Helps and supports women who have been raped
or sexually abused, no matter how long ago.

One-parent families

Gingerbread One Parent Families
Tel: 0800 018 5026 (9.15 a.m. to 5.15 p.m. week
days)
Advice and help with the problems faced by
single parents, including money, maintenance,
benefits and making friends.

National Council For One Parent Families
Tel: 0800 018 5026 (9.15 a.m. to 5.15 p.m.
weekdays)
Advice and help with the problems faced by
single parents, including money, maintenance
and benefits.

**National Council for the Divorce and
Separated**
Tel: 07041 478 120
Helps those divorced, separated or widowed look
towards a new beginning and a happier life.

If you are a young person

Childline
Tel: Freephone 0800 1111 (A free 24-hour service)
(Also free from BT Cellnet, One2One, Virgin and
Vodaphone)
Helpline for children and young people in the UK.

Get Connected
Tel: 0808 808 4994 or 0800 096 0096 (1 p.m. to
11 p.m. every day)
Helpline and referral service for anyone under 25.

Kidscape
Tel: 020 7730 3300 or 0845 120 5204 (10 a.m. to
4 p.m. weekdays)
For young people up to age 16.

Know Your Limits
Tel: 0800 917 8282 (24 hours)
Free alcohol advice aimed at young people.

Youth Access
Tel: 020 8772 9900 (office hours)
Counselling, information and support for young
people.

National Society for the Prevention of Cruelty to Children (NSPCC)
Tel: 0808 800 5000 (24 hours)
Help, advice and counselling for children and any adults worried about them.

15

Websites

The internet has become an invaluable resource for so many things and depression is no exception. The sites listed here are all reliable and range from those that will put you in touch with fellow sufferers to those that compile the latest research. However, it's always a good idea to compare information from at least three sites because, as in everything, opinions differ.

Depression (general)

www.aware.ie Information and support for people living in Ireland and Northern Ireland.
www.bacp.co.uk A list of counsellors in your area is available from the British Association for Counselling and Psychotherapy.
www.carelineuk.org Website for Careline which specializes in counselling those with depression and other difficulties.
www.cosca.org.uk Help from Counselling and Psychotherapy in Scotland.

www.dbsalliance.org Information and advice from the Depression and Bipolar Support Alliance.

www.deardenise.com Fact files about depression and other problems. Also inludes letters, a message board and Denise Robertson's thoughts on problems in the news.

www.depressionalliance.org Good site with plenty of information for sufferers and those who are living with them.

www.depressionanon.co.uk A country-wide mutual support group for sufferers.

www.depression.org.uk News, research and information from the charity Defeat Depression.

www.dipex.org/DesktopDefault.aspx Unusual and extremely useful website featuring people's personal experiences of illness in the form of written accounts and audio and video clips. If you're feeling depressed as a result of a medical problem there's plenty here to inform and inspire.

www.mentalhealth.org.uk If you want really detailed advice, research and news then this site from the Mental Health Foundation is the place to get it.

www.mind.org.uk This is a really excellent site with an enormous amount of helpful information from Mind, the mental health charity.

www.nhsdirect.nhs.uk Information from

theNational Health Service's NHS Direct.

www.nice.org.uk Guidelines for dealing with depression from the National Institute for Health and Clinical Excellence.

www.samaritans.org.uk Website for the Samaritans.

www.sane.org.uk SANE helps everybody affected by mental health problems.

http://en.wikipedia.org Online encyclopaedia written by anonymous contributors; extensive and generally reliable information about depression and its treatment.

www.wingofmadness.com Website dedicated to severe depression.

Bipolar disorder/manic depression

www.bipolarscotland.org.uk Information and self-help groups organized by the Bipolar Fellowship Scotland.

www.dbsalliance.org Information and advice from the US-based Depression and Bipolar Support Alliance.

www.mdf.org.uk Website of the Manic Depression Fellowship.

www.manicdepressionwales.org.uk Website of the Manic Depression Fellowship Wales.

Depression and antidepressants

www.dbsalliance.org Information and advice from the Depression and Bipolar Support Alliance.
www.depressionalliance.org Good site with plenty of information for sufferers and those who are living with them.
www.depressionanon.co.uk A country-wide mutual support group for sufferers.
www.depression.org.uk News, research and information from the charity Defeat Depression.
www.mind.org.uk Clear and regularly updated information and advice about antidepressants, side effects and withdrawal symptoms from Mind, the mental health charity.
www.rcpsych.ac.uk Brief but useful summary on antidepressants and many other topics from the Royal College of Psychiatrists.

Depression and psychotherapy

www.dbsalliance.org Information and advice from the Depression and Bipolar Support Alliance.
www.depressionalliance.org Good site with plenty of information for sufferers and those who are living with them.

www.depressionanon.co.uk A country-wide mutual support group for sufferers.

www.depression.org.uk News, research and information from the charity Defeat Depression.org.

http://easyweb.easynet.co.uk As the name suggests, easily understood descriptions of different therapies.

www.netdoctor.co.uk Clear explanations of the various different kinds of psychotherapy and much else.

www.rspsych.ac.uk Useful and dispassionate advice and information from the Royal College of Psychiatrists.

http://en.wikipedia.org Online encyclopaedia written by anonymous contributors; extensive and generally reliable information about psychotherapy and many other mental health topics.

Depression sanctuaries

www.maytree.org.uk Maytree is a charity that offers short stays in its North London house to those overcome by despair and suicidal thoughts.

Depression due to alcohol or drugs

www.al-anonuk.org.uk Website of Alcoholics
Anonymous.
www.ndh.org.uk Website of the National Drugs
Helpline.

Depression due to bereavement

www.crusebereavementcare.org.uk Advice and
support for those suffering from one of the
leading causes of depression.

Depression due to bullying

www.bullying.co.uk Masses of good advice and
ideas from the specialists on bullying.
www.childline.org.uk Advice and help from
Childline, one of the leading charities in the field.

Depression due to financial problems

www.clearstart.org Sound advice on debt
counselling, debt consolidation loans, individual
voluntary arrangements, bankruptcy and much
more.

Depression due to loneliness

www.federation-solo-clubs.co.uk The National
Federation of Solo Clubs represents about 150
singles clubs in the UK for those aged 25–65.
www.gingerbread.org.uk Help for single parents
via a website, helpline and local self-help groups.
www.ncds.org.uk National Council for the
Divorced and Separated. Also covers widows
and widowers.
www.thecalmzone.net Website of the Campaign
Against Living Miserably which helps men who
are isolated, depressed or suicidal.
www.work4travel.co.uk The website for those
seeking people to go on holiday with.

Depression during and after pregnancy

www.apni.org Information about postnatal
depression from the Association of Post Natal
Illness.
www.motherisk.org Information about the
effects of antidepressants and other medicines
during pregnancy and while breastfeeding.
www.pni-uk.com Website of Perinatal Illness –
UK, a charity specializing in psychological and
emotional problems during pregnancy and after.

Depression following relationship problems

www.marriagecare.org.uk Advice for couples in difficulties, backed up by 56 centres around the UK.

www.ncds.org.uk National Council for the Divorced and Separated.

www.nfm.u-net.com National Family Mediation which has local services to help couples in the process of separating. For Scotland see **www.familymediationscotland.org.uk**

www.relate.org.uk Advice from Relate, which deals with family, sexual and other relationship problems.

Depression due to seasonal affective disorder (SAD)

www.outsidein.co.uk Information and SAD products.

www.sada.org.uk Online advice from the UK-based SAD Association which, for a small fee, can also supply a detailed information pack.

www.sad-lighting.co.uk Useful advice and online catalogue of SAD lamps and related products.

Depression following sexual abuse

www.childline.org.uk Website for Childline
which helps youngsters in distress.
www.familymattersuk.org Website for men,
women and children who have suffered
childhood sexual abuse.
www.mosac.org.uk For mothers of sexually
abused children.
www.napac.org.uk Website of the National
Association for People Abused in Childhood.
www.nspcc.org.uk Website of the National
Society for the Prevention of Cruelty to Children.
www.rapecrisis.co.uk Website of the Rape
Crisis Federation.

Depression and young people

www.childline.org.uk The website for Childline
which helps children and teenagers in distress.
www.connexions.gov.uk Information for those
aged 13–19.
www.getconnected.org.uk Useful information
for the under-25s.
www.kidscape.org.uk Advice for children up to
age 16.

www.youthaccess.org.uk Search facility for counselling and advisory services throughout the UK.

Parents of depressed children

www.youngminds.org.uk Help for adults concerned about the mental health of a child.
www.oneparentfamilies.org.uk Advice and help if you're having to cope alone.
www.parentlineplus.org.uk Information for parents and others caring for depressed children.

16

Further reading

We've tried to make this book as comprehensive and easy to use as possible but if you'd like to learn more about any of the subjects here are some books that could help.

Generally helpful books

50 Things You Can Do Today to Beat Depression, Paul Vincent, Upfront Publishing, 2005.

Counselling for Toads: A Psychological Adventure, Robert De Board, Routledge 1998.

Depression: The Way Out Of Your Prison, Dorothy Rowe, Brunner-Routledge, 2003.

Feeling Good – The New Mood Therapy, David D. Burns, M.D., Avon Books, 1999.

How to Choose a Psychotherapist, Neville Symington, Karnac Books, 2003.

How to Lift Depression… Fast (The Human Givens Approach), Joe Griffin and Ivan Tyrrell, HG Publishing, 2004.

Malignant Sadness – The Anatomy of Depression, Lewis Wolpert, Faber and Faber, 1999.

Mind Over Mood: Cognitive Treatment Therapy Manual for Clients, Christine Padesky and Dennis Greenberger, Guilford Press, 1995.

Overcoming Depression, Paul Gilbert, Constable and Robinson, 2000.

Overcoming Low Self-Esteem, Melanie Fennell, Constable and Robinson, 1999.

Self-Coaching – How to Heal Anxiety and Depression, Joseph Luciani, John Wiley & Sons, 2001.

Shopping for a Shrink: A Simple Guide to Seeing a Counsellor Or Therapist, Todd Zemek, Wakefield Press, 2003.

Sunbathing in the Rain: A Cheerful Book About Depression, Gwyneth Lewis, HarperPerennial, 2006.

Teach Yourself Cognitive Behavioural Therapy, Aileen Milne, Hodder Education, 2007.

Undoing Depression: What Therapy Doesn't Teach You and Medication Can't Give You, Richard O'Connor, G. P. Putnam's Sons, 1999.

The Which Guide to Counselling and Therapy, Shamil Wanigaratne and Mike Brookes, Which? Books, 2003.

Addiction and depression

Addiction to alcohol, drugs, gambling, food and other things often goes hand-in-hand with depression.

Adolescent Drug and Alcohol Abuse: How to Spot it, Stop it and Get Help for Your Family, Nikki Babbit, O'Reilly 2000.

Alcoholics Anonymous – Big Book 4th Edition, AA Services, Hazelden Publishing, 2002.

The Easy Way to Stop Drinking: A Revolutionary New Approach to Escaping from the Alcohol Trap, Allen Carr, Sterling Publishing, 2005.

A Million Little Pieces, James Frey, John Murray, 2004.

No Big Deal – A Guide to Recovery from Addictions, Robert Lefever and John Coates, Sow's Ear Press, 2006.

Understanding Street Drugs: A Handbook Of Substance Misuse for Parents, Teachers and Other Professionals, David Emmett and Graeme Nice, Jessica Kingsley Publishers, 2005.

Alternative treatments

Awaken the Giant Within: How to Take Immediate Control of Your Mental, Emotional, Physical and Financial Life, Anthony Robbins, Pocket Books, 2001.

The Endorphin Effect, William Bloom, Piatkus, 2001.

Healing without Freud or Prozac: Natural Approaches to Curing Stress, Anxiety and Depression Wwithout Drugs and without Psychoanalysis, David Servan-Schreiber, Rodale International, 2005.

Natural Prozac: Learning to Release Your Body's Own Anti-Depressants, Joel Robertson and Tom Monte, HarperSanFrancisco, 1998.

Antidepressants

The Antidepressant Fact Book, Peter Roger Breggin, De Capo Press, 2001.

Coming off Antidepressants, Joseph Glenmullen, Constable Robinson, 2006.

Feeling Good – The New Mood Therapy, David D. Burns, M.D., Avon Books, 1999.

Your Drug May Be Your Problem: How and Why to Stop Taking Psychiatric Medications, Peter Roger Breggin and David Cohen, De Capo Press, 2000.

Financial problems and depression

Help – I Can't Pay My Bills, Sally Herigstad, St Martin's Griffin, 2006.
Money Mistakes You Can't Afford to Make: How to Solve Common Problems and Improve Your Personal Finances, Paul J. Lim, McGraw Hill Education, 2003.
Taking Stock: A Spiritual Guide to Rising Above Life's Financial Ups and Downs, Benjamin Blech, Amacom, 2003.

Living with a depressed person

Living with the Black Dog, Caroline Carr, White Ladder Press, 2007.

Life coaching

Teach Yourself Life Coach, Jeff Archer, Hodder Education, 2007.

Massage

The Complete Body Massage Course: An Introduction to the Most Popular Massage Therapies, Nicola Stewart, Collins & Brown, 2006. Comprehensive guide.

The New Complete Guide to Massage, Susan Mumford, Hamlyn, 2006.
Teach Yourself Massage, Denise Whichello Brown, Hodder Education, 2007.

Meditation

Insight Meditation Kit: A Step-By-Step Course on How to Meditate, Joseph Goldstein and Sharon Salzberg, Sounds True Audio, 2002.
The Meditation Bible – A Definitive Guide to Meditation for Every Purpose, Madonna Gauding, Godsfield Press, 2005.
Meditation for Beginners, Jack Kornfield, Bantam, 2005. Includes a CD.
Meditations for Personal Healing, Louise L. Hay, Hay House, 2005.
Audio book.
Teach Yourself Meditation, Naomi Ozaniec, Hodder Education, 2004. Meditation as a part of daily life.

Positive thinking

How to Stop Worrying and Start Living, Dale Carnegie, Vermilion, 1992.

Learn How to Think Positively, Glenn Harrold, Divinti Publishing, 2000.

Positive Thinking, Positive Action: Essential Steps to Achieve Your Potential, Douglas Miller, BBC Active, 2005.

The Power of Positive Thinking, Norman Vincent Peale, Wing Books, 1994.

The Promised Land: A Guide to Positive Thinking for Sufferers of Stress, Anxiety and Depression, Rick Norris, Author House, 2005.

Relaxation and stress

10 Simple Solutions to Worry: How to Calm Your Mind, Relax Your Body and Reclaim Your Life, Kevin Gyoerkoe and Pamela Wiegartz, New Harbinger, 2006.

1001 Ways to Relax: How to Beat Stress and Find Perfect Calm, Mike George, Duncan Baird, 2003.

Be Yourself: How to Relax and Take Control of Your Life, Lynda Field, Vermilion, 2003.

The Business of Learning to Relax, Celia Bibby, Bibby Publishing, 1999.

Teach Yourself Managing Stress, Terry Looker and Olga Gregson, Hodder Education, 2003.

Teach Yourself Relaxation, Richard Craze, Hodder Education, 2005.

Yoga

Teach Yourself Yoga, Mary Stewart, Hodder Education, 2003.

The Easy Yoga Workbook: The Perfect Introduction to Yoga, Tara Fraser, Duncan Baird, 2003.

The Yoga Bible: The Definitive Guide to Yoga Postures, Christina Brown, Godsfield Press, 2003.

Yoga for Pregnancy, Birth and Beyond, Francoise Freedman, Dorling Kindersley, 2004.

Yoga for You: A Step-By-Step Guide to Yoga at Home for Everybody, Tara Fraser, Duncan Baird, 2003.

Yoga Therapies: 45 Sequences to Relieve Stress, Depression, Repetitive Strain, Sports Injuries and More, Jessie Chapman and Dhyan, Ulysses Press, 2003.